Contents

Foreword

I don't know who first strung together those words—*A famous man is one whose children love him.* But the truth expressed haunts and inspires me.

Money, status, career, power, and a thousand other pursuits may burn brightly for a time in our lives. But when winds of reflection clear away the smoke, nothing satisfies or fulfills a man more profoundly than the genuine love and praise of his children.

For the past seven years, as editor and publisher of *Dads Only* newsletter, it has been my privilege to help fathers be more effective. Why dads give so little time and preparation to their most profound assignment in life remains to me a mystery. Children are the only earthly possession we can take to heaven.

One day while pondering the challenge of urging more fathers to greatness, I happened upon the idea of this book. The well-known men described herein were not chosen because they are more successful at fathering than you or I or thousands of other dads about whom we'll never read. They are here, first, because men of lesser fame may never have attracted your attention.

More importantly, they are here because of their commitment to being the most effective fathers they can be. Their insights, often learned the hard way, offer valuable help to your success as a dad.

It was my privilege to sit and talk at length about fathering with each of them. It was an added treat when half of them further agreed to be interviewed for a film/video series of the same title on fathering. To each I again express my gratitude.

All of the fathers in these chapters turn down many more worthy requests than they can accept. Each gave of his time in the sincere hope that what he has learned or the practices he follows might inspire and encourage you to greatness with your children.

In the arena of fathering, each of us wages his own battle. No one can replace us in our children's lives. Yet none of us needs struggle alone. Here are shouts of encouragement and a comforting embrace from fellow travelers who have also learned profound truths the hard way. To a man, each of these famous dads is pulling for you. And so am I.

Besides fame and fatherhood, one other thread weaves these twelve men together. Each recognizes children as a divine gift, and fathering as a sacred calling. Their family backgrounds span a wide spectrum. While some recall childhoods filled with love, others remember little besides heartache. Yet each believes he cannot be a successful father today without the enablement of God's Spirit.

When considering fathers and fame, I am drawn back to God, the most famous of fathers. Like every dad, he longs for the affectionate obedience and daily praise of each of his children. So again, with childlike wonder I pray, "Father, I love you."

—Paul Lewis

FAMOUS FATHERS

Paul Lewis
and Dave Toht

David C. Cook Publishing Co.

Dedication

*To committed fathers everywhere, but especially to Billy
Lewis—a man who has encouraged, corrected, and
counseled me; the one who more than any other has loved
me and modeled to me a compassionate manliness worth
following. To the most famous father I know—my dad.*

A famous man is one whose children love him.

David C. Cook Publishing Company, Elgin, Illinois 60120
David C. Cook Publishing Company, Weston, Ontario
FAMOUS FATHERS
© 1984 by Paul Lewis

Photo Credits   Neville Bell   William Cornelia
David K. Holmes   Paul Lewis   London Sunday Mirror   Ake
Lundberg   Norman Seef   Dave Toht   Dave Valdez, The White House

First printing, 1984
Printed in the United States of America
89 88 87 86 85 84   5 4 3 2 1

Library of Congress Cataloging in Publication Data •
Lewis, Paul, 1944-
   Famous fathers.
   1. Fathers—United States—Biography. 2. Father and child—United
States—Addresses, essays, lectures.
I. Toht, David. II. Title.
HQ756.L48 1984   306.8'742'0922   84-17586
ISBN 0-89191-657-1

ROSEY GRIER

*P*arents must be consistently truthful. You can't run games on kids. You must be honest with them and tell them the truth and let the truth stand.

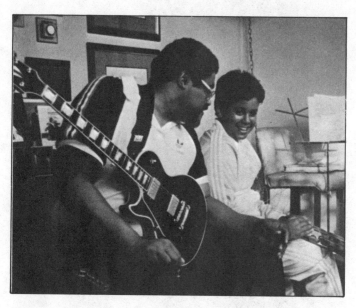

ROSEY GRIER
Rosey and his son, Rosey, Jr., enjoy their close father-son
relationship.

Rosey Grier was there the June night in 1968 when Robert Kennedy was shot. At the Los Angeles Ambassador Hotel, Senator Kennedy had just delivered a victory speech after impressively winning the California Democratic presidential primary. As a family friend and political supporter, Rosey was escorting Ethel Kennedy through the kitchen corridor of the hotel.

Suddenly a shot rang out. Rosey pushed Ethel to the floor and rushed the assailant. Taking charge in the confusion, he twisted the gun out of Sirhan Sirhan's hand and then pinned him to one of the stainless steel serving tables. As the crowd surged around them, Rosey arched over Sirhan, fending off angry blows.

Such is the stuff Rosey Grier is made of. As a defensive tackle for the New York Giants and then one of the famous "fearsome foursome" for the Los Angeles Rams, Rosey earned the reputation of a gentle giant who could get the job done.

A torn Achilles tendon ended his

career. But this shy kid from Georgia quickly turned to music and acting. And not being a man guided much by stereotypes, he even authored a successful book about one of his favorite pastimes—needlepoint. America's own Renaissance man was very much in demand.

But there was another side to Rosey Grier's life—a daughter born out of wedlock, a failed first marriage, and a selfish concern with his own personal fulfillment that kept his life out of balance and led to a second divorce.

It was ultimately fatherhood that led Rosey out of the dark. The catalyst was his son, Rosey, Jr. Through his love for his son, a significant renewal of his relationship with God took place, and Rosey began repairing the broken relationships of his life—including remarrying Margie, his second wife and Rosey, Jr.'s, mom.

Today, Rosey Grier is committed to the importance and challenge of being a father. And like every dad who pays attention, he has received more than he has given.

Rosey Grier and ten-year-old Rosey, Jr., were wrestling. As the aggressive horseplay escalated, Rosey, Sr., deftly pinned his big-for-his-age son to the carpet. Contemplating the hulk of a dad looming over him, Rosey, Jr., scarcely missed a beat before bravely declaring, "All right, Dad, I've got you right where I want you."

In the give-and-take of this father/son duo, Rosey, Jr., has been the catalyst for the most important changes in Rosey's life. Without these course corrections, he would have arrived at a far different and less desirable destination. Grier's experience affirms the truth that in parenting, fathers frequently grow as much as their children. Love, responsibility, and the sometimes mysterious ways of God have put Rosey right where he needed to be.

When Rosey's wife, Margie, first announced that she was pregnant, he was admittedly less than enthusiastic. Behind him was a sterling string of achievements, each belying his humble roots as the seventh of eleven children born to poor Georgia farmers.

Rosey recalls once telling his dad he would work the whole year for a dollar and felt that would be *"some* money." Now he could reflect on pro football stardom first with the New York Giants and then with the Los Angeles Rams, popularity as a television and motion picture star, political involvement with America's national heroes, and an impressive record of public service with young people from the most deprived sections of Los Angeles. Ahead of him stretched an expanding world of shining career possibilities. So Rosey Grier didn't want the burden of new responsibilities. "I didn't even jump up and down," he recalls. "I felt like, boy, I'm trapped."

When Margie gave birth to a son, the elation Rosey felt surprised him. "I thought I was going to be so cool, but I leaped into the air," he says. "From that day on, my life changed."

Rosey became a doting dad, racing to be first to respond to his new son's cries, forgetting that he had told Margie he didn't intend to touch the baby for at least six months. This six-foot-five, 280-pound man found himself tenderly cradling this tiny treasure, changing his diapers, giving him baths, and stealing him away to show him off to friends.

Ironically, the more the father-son relationship deepened, the more Rosey's marriage seemed to falter. The love was gone. Rosey came to feel he had outgrown it. Even this marvelous child couldn't hold them together. When Rosey, Jr., was five years old, Dad and Mom got a divorce.

Fortunately, both Rosey and Margie were wise enough to know that they couldn't use Rosey, Jr., to hurt the other without hurting him. So while there was little trust, each treated the other "nice."

T he court decided that Rosey, Jr., would live with his mom and stay every other weekend with his dad. And it was during one of those visits that Rosey, Jr., asked the inevitable question, "Dad, why did you have to get divorced?" Attempting to reassure the obviously vulnerable child, he said, "Your mom and I, we don't get along. But it ain't nothing to do with you. We both love you."

"Then little Rosey said, 'Dad, I don't think you should do it.' And that broke me up. He was so innocent." The child became the epoxy that kept Rosey and Margie in touch and occasionally talking with each other. "If it wasn't for little Rosey," he says, "we would have never made it. There was that calm around him."

Once while at Rosey's apartment, Margie offered to help clean the place and came across a paper on which Rosey had written down the kind of person he wanted to be: one who loved God, who loved his son, and whose son loved him. Margie started crying and said, "I don't fit in there." To which Rosey responded, "You? You fit in there? It's over, man. That's not you. No, of course, you don't fit there."

T hen, by an odd set of circumstances, Rosey, Jr., provided the means of healing the marriage. It began when a friend called one Sunday morning and convinced Rosey to watch a television evangelist. He began viewing the program regularly, and one week the minister preached on John 3:16. "When I heard *eternal life* it triggered something inside of me," Rosey recalls.

"When I was divorced from my wife, I began to want to teach my son a prayer that would always give him comfort—the Lord's Prayer. So that morning I called my ex-wife and said, 'Listen, Margie. There is a man on TV I want you and little Rosey to watch.'"

In their separate homes, listening to the Word of God became a regular part of their Sunday morning routines. Then one Sunday little Rosey, who had never been to church before, asked Rosey to take him. At the end of the service, the minister invited those who wanted to ask Jesus into their lives to raise their hands. Rosey, Sr.'s, hand went up followed by Rosey, Jr.'s. Both were born again that day.

One weekend soon after, little Rosey asked, "Dad, can we take Mom to church?" Rosey recalls, "I thought, oh, my, no, oh, no. I don't think so. I stalled, saying, 'Well, sometime.' He said, 'Why not tomorrow?' I didn't have a 'why not' answer, so I invited her." She accepted Christ.

Family trips to the services became a regular Sunday event. Almost without realizing it, another miracle was in the making.

One Sunday I brought them both back home, and we were sitting talking," says Rosey. "I couldn't believe what Margie was saying. She sounded real nice. I asked her, 'Did you ever talk to me like that?' She responded, 'Yeah, why?' I said, 'Well, you sure sound good.' I realized that I really did care for her. Eventually I told her I loved her, and I asked her to marry me again."

A love kindled by Rosey, Jr., had again gotten his dad "right where he wanted him."

The Griers' newfound Christian faith and resulting desire to build up their family drew Rosey into a new commitment to fathering. He reflected a lot on his own upbringing in an effort to do the best possible job of being a parent.

One of Rosey's most embarrassing—and instructive—childhood memories concerns the time he had to sell watermelons. The family was never rich and always had to work hard. One day, his dad had him ride in their mule-driven wagon through a small, nearby Georgia town shouting, "Watermelon, get your watermelon!" It seemed to Rosey demeaning and humiliating. "I wanted to hide underneath the seat, anyplace, just to get out of it," he says.

Why it had to be done and why his family needed the money were not explained to young Rosey. He feels now that had the reason for the task been explained, he wouldn't have found it so difficult to help out. And that experience has influenced his own approach.

"I think we blindly tell our kids, do this, do that, but we don't explain why," he says. "We should tell them why we have been doing certain things so that they have an understanding of the importance."

An example from his football days illustrates this belief. Coaches

12

used to urge Rosey to play "madder" as a lineman. They would try to get him angry, thinking it would help him play harder. "I wanted to play my best, but I didn't want to hurt anyone," he says. "I could see through what they were doing. Had my coaches shared with me why they wanted me to get tougher, I would have let go."

Besides explaining why certain conduct is necessary, Rosey knows a father must set the tone by his own example. He emphasizes that living one's beliefs is the primary way to guide children—mainly because kids pay close attention to what their parents do.

"I guarantee that every child is totally aware of his parents even though he might act totally contrariwise," asserts Rosey. "Parents

"It's my goal that my son won't have to unlearn anything, because we've started him out right."

must show a consistent love by their actions and also must be consistently truthful. You can't run games on kids. You must be honest with them and tell them the truth and let the truth stand. It is the only thing that eventually will come back to them that they will be able to stand on."

This principle relates to behavior at school as well as at home. Rosey is convinced that parents can't afford to depend on the teacher for intellectual and moral growth. He demands of himself parental involvement. "Parents are setting a tremendous hurdle for their kids if they don't really watch them," he believes. "The parents ought to be involved in what the kids are learning and studying. They should share with them, question them about what they're learning—not just let the teacher take care of them.

"Personal growth requires a context in which goals can be set and some sort of structure established that keeps us working toward these goals. Kids, no less than adults, often set ambitious goals only to drop them once the going gets tough."

Rosey has watched his son develop a lot of interests ranging from drums to piano to art and, with more regularity, to basketball and football. And while encouraging his son in each, Rosey has realized that Rosey, Jr.'s, enthusiasm was short lived. "Now when he wants to do something I say, 'Okay, you must master it, otherwise we don't do it. You've got to stay on it until you're good enough at it.' Right now he's practicing tennis. I told him, 'When you can beat me, you can quit.' "

Rosey disciplines his son both by increasing what he expects of him and by taking away certain things from him. And being the bright and naturally inquisitive child Rosey, Jr., is, he tends to start more projects than he can finish. "He doesn't want to work at anything yet," observes Rosey.

"My path now is to try to get him to where he really works at something to get it right. I try to show him, to motivate him to do it. I don't want to force him, but I want him to be motivated to do stuff. And my emphasis is always upon learning the fundamentals of whatever he's trying to learn."

Rosey credits his own childhood on a farm with teaching him the disciplines of hard work. Farming demanded that every member of the family, even the very young, participate in the chores. There was no artificial disciplinary structure—what needed to be done, had to be done. "As a kid, I was up working at five in the morning and then walked ten miles to school. It bothers me that Rosey, Jr., hardly has to do any work at all. I want him to get the skill of being consistent—not to get high about something and then fall off."

A mong the values Rosey hopes to instill in his son are honesty, concern, confidence in his faith, and an ability to love and care for others. "He has some good directions," says Rosey. "It takes consistency in trying to help him get these things down. But I realize it takes time to grow that way. It's my goal that he won't have to unlearn anything because we've started him out right."

Bible study receives a lot of emphasis in the Grier home. Rosey is an avid reader of religious and devotional works, portions of which he shares with his family. And Rosey, Jr., often reads out loud from the Bible to his dad.

"I also watch his prayer development," says Rosey. "I try to listen to his praying and then teach him how to pray. I'm just a youngster, too, in my knowledge of who I am in Christ. So it's good for both of us."

Keeping the family close and in communication is a definite

priority. Bible study and prayer have provided not only a means of guidance for the family, but have facilitated the sharing of thoughts and concerns. "Every morning we join together in speaking about the day, what we have to do that day, and pray to God for the opportunity to serve him."

Still in great demand as a speaker, Rosey sometimes regrets the travel it requires, especially when he feels his son needs him at home. "We need to talk more than we have been," he says. "I think that at times I begin to feel him slipping away a little bit—not in terms of love, but because he's more involved with his friends."

Rosey called a family meeting on the subject of his traveling to tell his son how sorry he was that he would have to be away so much. "Little Rosey said to me, 'Well, Dad, you got to be a cheerful giver.' So, I go out knowing that we're still together."

Rosey Grier is a big man in heart, stature, and experience. He finds himself growing daily as he guides his family. Having often been in the company of superstars, a White House guest many times over, and one who has tasted of multiplied success, he knows how to distinguish between reality and life's counterfeits.

"If there was anything in it, some of it should have touched my deepest needs, shouldn't it?" he asks. "I was impressed by all that. But it didn't show me that it was the answer to what I was looking for." Once Jesus Christ and his love took hold, Rosey knew his greatest accomplishment would be one well within the reach of every father.

"It's a man's responsibility to make sure he is leading his family in the right direction," says Rosey. "Many men go the other way and let their wives bring up the family. To build a family on the love of God is the greatest thing any man can do."

CHUCK SWINDOLL

I want to leave them with a strong sense of self-worth and confidence. If I'm gone out of their life tomorrow, their lasting memory will be, "Here's a man who believed in me and was committed to my future even if it were very different from his.

CHUCK SWINDOLL
At family gatherings of three generations of Swindolls,
Chuck enjoys his new role of grandfather, as well as his
ongoing role of dad.

His mom liked music—good music and singing quartets with the kids. So at age four, Chuck Swindoll was the tenor; six-year-old Luci, the alto; seven-year-old Orville, the base; and Mom was the soprano.

A few years later, with World War II making headlines, the tunes they sang were patriotic, punctuated by folk songs and crazy ditties for fun. They would sing at various gatherings, but Chuck remembers singing his best in Red Helberczak's El Campo, Texas, drugstore. The customers applauded. And ole Red, he would pay . . . with scoops of ice cream!

Forty-six years later, Chuck Swindoll is the contented father of four. The First Evangelical Free Church of Fullerton, California, where he is senior pastor, has experienced explosive growth. In addition, his ministry extends around the world through the extensive distribution of messages on cassette tape and via "Insight for Living," a thirty-minute daily radio broadcast aired more than seven hundred times each day.

Though the complex pattern of life today belies Chuck's simple childhood, the threads remain the same—authenticity, practicality, relevance, efficiency, and following through. These emphases permeate his fathering agenda. "My greatest announcement to the world is really my kids," he says. "I think that makes or breaks what I talk about."

Chuck's mom was the creative and determined figure who kept their Houston, Texas, family moving. Dad was a machinist, a God-fearing, somewhat reserved man. Grandfather Lundy was the one who really influenced Chuck's early life with fishing trips and memorable times at a little bay cottage.

Chuck recalls heading out to play football one day when his mom revealed a promise she held for him from the Book of Proverbs. The slip pinned up on the wall above the kitchen sink read, "A man's gift makes room for him and brings him before great men." Much later it would take the loving confidence and encouragement of his wife Cynthia to bring that simple prophecy to life.

In high school Chuck stuttered until a drama teacher's affirmation helped him begin speaking without fear. His decision to become a Christian pastor developed much later during a tour of duty with the Marine Corps in the Orient.

Although Chuck graduated from Dallas Theological Seminary with three major honors, it has been his gift for clear, accurate, and life-related exposition of Scripture which has spawned his tremendous popularity. His nearly two dozen best-selling inspirational books and booklets reveal an unusual insight into the needs of hurting people.

Chuck Swindoll avoids taking the notoriety of his ministry and himself too seriously. He'd much rather talk about the new challenge of being a father to adult children and his recent induction as a grandfather. Now, fifty-two pounds lighter than four years ago (when he began running every morning), he has the energy to do it.

*I*had overbooked myself," recounts Chuck Swindoll, about an unforgettable weekend some time ago. "I was irritable and feisty, so I nailed one of the kids at the table. They answered back and I set them straight. My wife, Cynthia, frowned in my direction, so I commenced to deal with her. My oldest son, Curt, slammed down his napkin and walked out. I began to shake, I was so embarrassed—so under pressure and intense." Was this indeed the "friendly, perceptive presence" so familiar to Chuck's radio audience five days a week on "Insight for Living"?

In the Swindoll home, Saturday mornings are usually reserved for coffee, donuts, and good family talk. This one was different. Chuck was overextended. It was Easter weekend. Besides Sunday's services to prepare for, there was a banquet to emcee and another speaking engagement. Then first thing Monday morning Chuck was booked to catch a flight to a seminary board meeting out of state.

Several things were signaling the need for some family patching up: "I can count on one hand the number of times anybody has ever stomped out of a disagreement in our place, because we're just not stompers," Chuck continued. "We'll slug it out verbally, but we don't walk out and leave it. And when I sensed Cynthia's strong disagreement with me in front of the children, I knew I was in need. That day I needed that kind of frown.

*F*inally, I noticed that most everybody was in tears. They were quiet out of fear of me. I realized I had lost at that moment a great deal of what I'd spent years trying to gain—a respectful kind of authority. I had to decide if I was going to handle this as a servant or just tighten my lips, tighten my belt—demand that they get the dishes done, and get this place clean. I could just skate off to another meeting."

Chuck chose to take the servant role. He canceled every weekend commitment he could and cleared the slate for the rest of the day. The Swindoll family took the afternoon to do some overdue emotional housecleaning.

"I got everybody together upstairs," Chuck remembers, "—except for Curt who had gone to his weekend job. We sat around on the floor, kind of powwow style. We cried and we confessed and we forgave."

It was a memorable day for the whole family—the day each of the children learned that when the bottom falls out of family relationships and somebody has to give, sometimes that somebody is Dad!

When the family conference ended, one piece of unfinished business remained. Away at his part-time job, Curt had not been included in the family reconciliation. So that evening Chuck drove the whole family to where Curt was cleaning an office building.

*H*e had been to several buildings and was on his last one," Chuck recalls. "Curt met us at the door with tears welling up in his eyes, and he said, 'I'm having such a hard day.' I pulled him up close to me and we walked inside. We spent the next hour working it through and building back the bridges. We all helped him finish the cleanup and then we went down to Denny's and topped it off with supper together." It was one of the Swindoll family's finest hours.

Chuck's concern for a supportive family has its roots in his own childhood. Though his was a tight-knit family ("We were a clannish bunch—you couldn't break into the Swindoll tribe too easily"), he understands what it means to a kid not to receive all the love and support that might ideally be desired. "I think I felt a little less affirmed and loved than my older brother and sister," he says. "In my childhood eyes my mom's favorite child was my brother and my dad's favorite was my sister. I was unplanned. I did not have a quick brain like my brother. He was very bright— I.Q. approaching genius. My sister was multitalented. And then I came along."

Chuck feels his parents expended their best efforts on the older children. His dad worked the three-to-eleven shift as a machinist and was not around in the key evening hours when most family interaction takes place.

"In my childhood eyes, my mom's favorite child was my brother and my dad's favorite was my sister. I was unplanned."

"I missed his counsel," Chuck says. "I guess I missed most my father's affirmation. It's hard to say that today because I loved my folks. But I could count on two hands the number of times both of them ever came to something I was involved in—like drama,

24

music, or sports. That's why I think it is so important for me to be with my children and tell them what I think they do right."

Certainly the effect on Chuck was not overwhelmingly negative. It just set him back a bit in finding his bearings in life. "I didn't know where I could contribute," he reflects. "When I got out of high school, I just slipped into what my dad had been doing and went to work in the machine shop where he was the superintendent. I went to night school at the University of Houston, but I lacked clear direction regarding goals and objectives."

A two-year stint in the Marines began to hone some of Chuck's leadership skills and, more importantly, provided the climate during which he gained the strong desire to give himself to Christian ministry as a pastor. Chuck says he joined the Marines because its image of building men was in keeping with his mom's conviction that, "If you're going to do it, get into something worth having. Never settle for less than the best!"

Still, Chuck did not receive the support he really needed. "I am somewhat of a stranger to affirmation. The first person I can remember who really affirmed me was a drama teacher in high school who believed in me when I stuttered. He helped me when I was feeling like a wallflower and gave me the ability to speak in public with confidence." Over the years since then, the greatest affirmation has come from Cynthia. "She has believed in me when I didn't really even believe in myself. I play that record at times when I am a little unsure. I play those words, 'You can do it. You're one of the best, if not the best . . . certainly the best in this situation.' "

While their paths didn't cross as much as Chuck would have liked, he credits his father with two great legacies. One was a clean, morally pure life-style. "It never dawned on me that my father had one thought of unfaithfulness. And the modeling of purity of lips even though he worked around men that were vile and obscene really stuck." The second was how to treat a wife. "He really did honor my mom. I watched that on weekends. There were times they would have their rows, but I don't remember his ever raising his voice and certainly never his hand. So, I gained that kind of tenderness and consistency."

Chuck began fathering as a hard-charging dad who, when one of the kids had been assigned to do the lawn, would point out each of the areas that had been missed. "Now when my kids mow the lawn it's a thrill to say, 'Young man, you handled that well,' rather than to pick out the oversights."

Swindoll's fathering style indeed has changed over the years. He has come to view things from his children's point of view. "I think the oldest child often gets the raw deal in most families. We overexpect and overdiscipline."

While his earlier parenting efforts were aimed at molding the behavior of his kids, his primary emphasis now is to affirm them and to build them up. "I want to leave them with a strong sense of self-worth and confidence," he says. "If I'm gone out of their life tomorrow, their lasting memory will be, 'Here's a man who believed in me and was committed to my future even if it were very different from his.' "

The overarching goal, then, is that all four of his children become all they're meant to be. And Chuck avoids conjuring up a hidden agenda for them. He honestly would be equally pleased whether they became Ph.D.s or never finished college and worked with their hands, say in a construction crew or woodshop. Such a perspective frees him from forcing them into a mold for which they may not be suited. It takes away the pressure of their having to become something for the sake of his image.

Frankly, this comes with difficulty for a man who is a self-admitted disciplinarian and high achiever, and likes to make every minute of his day count. By Chuck's account, "I hit the floor running. When I wake up in the morning, I'm awake—I mean instantly." He doesn't like red lights or haircuts or anything else that "slows me down or wastes time." He habitually backs into parking places—"because you're usually not in a big hurry to come in, but you're often in a big hurry to get out."

And such is the pace of his working day. "However, when evening comes," says Chuck, "I'm a fireplace kind of guy. If we could afford only a one-room home, I would have a fireplace in that one room. I've been tempted to turn on the air conditioning to make it comfortable enough to have a fire in the fireplace around which we can talk and share the events of the day. I don't know how many times we've gone to sleep by a fire popping in our old Franklin stove. I've awakened and carried the kids to bed at two or three in the morning."

Warm family times such as these underline Chuck's preference for the support and excitement of a large family. And the kids like it, too. When Charissa, Chuck's older daughter, became a summer camp counselor, she chose to work with high schoolers. And Colleen, her younger sister, spontaneously requested—in fact, demanded—that she be placed in Charissa's cabin. "Because I want to be with her and I want her to be my leader," she stated.

With four kids, the Swindoll family forms its own support group. "In our family you have the extremes of all kinds of personalities. You have a broader spectrum, like a windshield wiper. We've had a chance to see a lot of interplay and to discover, for example, a lot of in-house, unplanned support and love." Chuck will often ask an only child the question, "Does 'only' always rhyme with 'lonely'?" One responded, "It did in my case. I was very lonely and felt ripped off. I wanted that interplay with a brother or sister."

Chuck believes these days that fathers seeking to guide their children toward the right life-style are often bewildered by the myriad of new options that have been spawned in the last forty years. "They've long struggled with television, but must now deal with video games, home computers, frightening music, affluence, mobility, sexual irresponsibility—all those factors we rightly or wrongly blame when kids take the wrong path. Much of this has to do merely with handling some of the new tools technology has provided us with. But a great deal of it concerns a brand-new set of moral assumptions—assumptions that are subtle and contrary to Christianity."

So the question must be asked, "In view of the radically different climate in which our children are growing up, are fathers correct in guiding their families by old patterns?"

"I don't want to raise a family of dated children," Chuck adds quickly. "It's not my desire to have them spend the rest of their lives longing for the days of the sixties and seventies when life was such and such. I would hope that character will be forever their highest priority." Chuck doesn't want his children to avoid the risk of change of the modern world. Rather, he hopes they will continue to be in touch with the mainstream of humanity and not retreat to the safety of some distant and historic mountaintop of yesteryear. "Staying in touch with real people and real needs will do more to keep us relevant than anything I know about."

Chuck finds much that is desirable in popular culture and some things that are undesirable. For the Swindolls, good films become family events and spark long discussions. Books and music also form an important part of family life.

Within their family, tastes differ—especially in music. So they have a rule aimed at maintaining a good balance between personal freedom and family sanity. "If it's hurting or bothering another person in our family who is trying to be reasonable about it, then it isn't fair to push it on them. If you turn the volume down enough to where you can enjoy it, fine. But if it's not to my taste, don't force me to listen to it."

Chuck is not enamored with video games. "Who wants to relate to a box that beeps and clinks and rewards you with a free game?" But he is cautious in responding to a son who likes few things more than buying new video game cartridges. "I'm not too thrilled with that. But then, maybe he isn't too thrilled that I can watch the Cowboys play football for three hours."

The Swindoll kids are now beginning to leave the nest to strike out on their own. Both Curtis and Charissa are now happily married. And recently Curt presented Chuck and Cynthia with a grandson, Ryan Swindoll, born on Christmas morning, 1983!

Looking back on the job he has done as a father thus far, Chuck notes, "I find myself thinking, 'How do I father a child out of the nest?' It's a new thing. We all think we can do that before it happens. But when it comes it's a strange thing. It's funny, but I'm kind of fearful—afraid of doing the wrong thing maybe more than ever because Cynthia and I don't want to lose their friendship and respect. Of great importance is our need to maintain a healthy and well-exercised sense of humor. This enables us to keep a clear perspective on life.

"The other day I called Curt to wish him a happy birthday, and I found myself saying, 'I'm proud of you. I think you've got so many things in life together.' I felt free to say a lot of very personal things. They weren't written on paper somewhere: 'Call Curt on Friday, and say . . .' I want to affirm him and the others now more than ever. I want my children to reach the full potential of who they're meant to be. Cynthia and I want to do everything we can possibly do to help them accomplish their objectives.

Similarly, I respect their mother's feelings about their future now more than ever. I see her as wiser than I've ever seen her. And I'm telling her that. She is the executive director of the Insight for Living ministry and the success she has made of that role has generated in me enormous feelings of pride. I realize now the magnitude of the contribution she has made to my children. I'm saying, 'I'm so glad they had a mother who balanced out some of my weaknesses, and affirmed or underlined some of my strengths.' We talk more frequently about the kids as the years go by, and I think we see life behind their eyes better than we ever have."

Chuck is fond of Sara Teasdale's grand poem which he learned from his sister, Luci. In a piece entitled "Wisdom" she writes:

When I have ceased to break my wings
Against the faultiness of things,
And learned that compromises wait
Behind each hardly opened gate,
When I can look Life in the eyes,
Grown calm and very coldly wise,
Life will have given me the Truth,
And taken in exchange—my youth.*

"That's what's happening to me," Chuck reflects. "I'll be fifty shortly, but I feel myself getting older if for no other reason than the kids are leaving. Not old like ornery Norm Thayer in 'On Golden Pond,' but old like that piece of verse—life has taken my youth, but in exchange, it's given me the truth. I am now more objective than I've ever been. And in all honesty I'm no different than other dads in that I wish I could do some of it over again."

But through a knowing smile he adds, "Dadgummit, I can't."

Reprinted with permission of Macmillan Publishing Company from *Collected Poems* by Sara Teasdale. © 1917 by Macmillan Publishing Co., Inc., renewed 1945 by Mamie T. Wheless.

KEN COOPER

There's no way I can keep my body in shape unless I practice at least three, four, or five times a week. Family relationships are exactly the same. You can't store them. Like exercise, they're an ongoing type of thing.

KEN COOPER
Ken, his wife, and their two children make outdoor activities an integral part of their lives.

In 1968, Dr. Kenneth Cooper went to Brazil to help the Flamingo Club of Rio de Janeiro soccer team develop an aerobics program to perfect their performance. Using his system, they brought the World Cup back to Brazil in 1970. Overnight, aerobics became popular, making Dr. Cooper an instantaneous hero.

The word *aerobics* didn't translate well into Portuguese, so the program became known as "The Cooper." And today, when a Brazilian wants to know if you've been jogging, he'll ask, "Have you done your Cooper?"

For nearly twenty years, thanks to the dogged determination of its creator, Ken Cooper, aerobic exercise has kept multiplied millions of people healthier and happier.

Dr. Cooper's books, including *Aerobics, The New Aerobics, The Aerobics Way, Aerobics for Women,* and *The Aerobics Program for Total Well Being,* have sold more than twelve million copies in twenty-four languages plus Braille. He has lectured in every state and to the medical and sports elite of the world.

For this father of two, balancing the excitement of his work and the joys of his family presents a daily challenge. He copes with nonstop pressures at the Aerobics Center, his thirty-acre fitness development facility in north Dallas, Texas. There he presides over aerobics research and programs while remaining the personal physician to many of America's top business and sports figures.

This dynamo of a man, raised in a dentist's home in Oklahoma City and intent as a collegian on becoming a medical missionary, is obviously a man with a mission— to popularize preventive medicine.

Cooper conducted his original aerobics research as a Senior Flight Surgeon and Lt. Colonel in the Air Force Medical Corps. Today aerobics remains the official fitness program of the United States Air Force and the Navy. His exercise program also is followed in over five hundred schools throughout the United States and by many professional and collegiate athletic teams.

Annually Dr. Cooper lectures some one hundred times in behalf of his compelling conviction that "it is much cheaper and more effective to maintain good health than it is to regain it once it is lost."

In 1977 Dr. Cooper was recipient of the Daniel Webster Award given for the "most important speech on the most important problems facing the U.S. and its citizens." The accolade joined scores of others he has been awarded, including a Presidential Citation and Congressional Distinguished Service Award.

At times the applause leaves breathless even a man in Ken Cooper's condition. But the fame he enjoys most is the esteem in which he is held by his wife, Millie, eighteen-year-old daughter, Berkeley, and thirteen-year-old son, Tyler.

*T*o wake up at seven in the morning, have a leisurely breakfast, read the newspaper, get to the office at nine, be home by quarter to six, take a swim, play with the kids, have dinner, and go to bed at ten thirty—all that seems very utopian to me," muses Dr. Ken Cooper. "Personally, I think I'd be bored. There's a tendency in me to put work at the top of my priorities."

Ken Cooper loves his work. At age fifty-three, he is one of the rare individuals who, if given the chance to do anything he wanted to do in life, would choose exactly what he's doing now—performing with aplomb in five separate areas: practicing physician, lecturer, author, president of the Institute for Aerobics Research, and owner-director of the Aerobics Center.

He may find himself on a book promotional tour this week, off to lend his influence and share his Christian testimony at a South American missionary crusade the next, and then home again to supervise research and development at his Dallas Aerobics Center. To compensate for such a schedule, Ken Cooper has been forced to exclude some activities common to many to allow him time with his wife, Millie, daughter, Berkeley, and son, Tyler.

"There are things we feel we have to sacrifice," he says. "We have no regular social life. We have few friends we can consistently associate with. I'd love to spend time with Roger and Marianne Staubach and people like them whom we know well and see professionally all the time. But when you spend so much time at work and so much time traveling, what time you do have you want to spend with your family. And I don't spend as much time with my family as most fathers do," admits Ken. "It's prohibitive with the type of life that I live. But I think that the family has gained tremendously as a result of my activities."

Ken is in constant demand as a speaker—averaging about one hundred lectures a year. Many offer enviable opportunities to travel. And whenever appropriate, Millie or Berkeley and Tyler go along with him.

When my son was starting kindergarten," Ken recalls, "the teacher went around the room asking the children what they did during the summer months. When she got to Tyler, who was very articulate at five, he said, 'Well, we started off by going to Hawaii, and then we went to the Olympics in Montreal, and then we went to Tahiti. . . .' The teacher, who I am sure had never been out of Texas and Oklahoma, didn't believe what my son said. So she called my wife, Millie, who had to assure her, 'Yes, that's where he was this summer.' "

Family priorities serve as a kind of throttle on Ken's travel schedule. Sundays are guarded as family days. When home, they attend services at First Baptist Church in Dallas. And on occasion Ken teaches an adult Sunday school class. He accepts no speaking engagements for the month of December, and in July and August will take only speaking commitments to which his family is also invited. In the down times, a Colorado mountain retreat they built with another family forms a regular backdrop to many of their warmest family memories.

His wife, Millie, an accomplished speaker in her own right and coauthor with Ken of *The Aerobics Woman*, travels with him. It's a point of special sensitivity for Cooper, who has witnessed the identity crises common to wives in the shadows of highly visible professional men—crises which he has often seen lead to divorce or even suicide.

Thus, Ken has encouraged Millie to develop and express her own considerable talents in areas beyond their home. And over the years, at those times when she has joined Ken on the road, her parents have come to stay in the Cooper home with the grandkids—keeping Tyler and Berkeley very secure under the extended-family umbrella.

Ken worries that what his children might most remember about him thus far is that "Dad was too busy." Usually he's up at 5:45 in the morning and not asleep before midnight—regularly logging sixty-hour workweeks.

"We do try to have good, quality family time," Ken says. And he wisely recognizes that only time will accurately judge whether his strategies to compensate for his time away from his family were truly successful.

"I'm changing," Cooper says. "I'm really trying, because these are very critical years. A night ago when I was working on my newest book, I was transferring some information from a little thirty-five-millimeter slide to paper. I couldn't read it without a magnifying glass. So I said, 'Ty, come on in here.' He came in and was reading off the numbers for me. Later I heard him say to Berkeley, 'I got to help Daddy write his book.' And that was something. I didn't realize it was so important to him."

Ken Cooper comes from a long line of self-motivated achievers. His grandfather was an itinerant Baptist preacher, known to accept a twenty-five dollar honorarium for preaching at a country church, only to turn around and put twenty dollars back in the offering

Ken worries *that what his children might most remember about him is "Dad was too busy."*

plate. Ken's dad was a dentist who put himself through school, built a thriving dental practice, and maintained the family tradition of working long, hard hours.

"My dad left early in the morning before I woke up and never got home until after dark," Ken recalls. "But on his afternoons off and a lot of times on Sunday after church, we'd go out to a farm he had bought about an hour from our home. Dad and I would feed the calves . . . feed the cattle. So I was raised in kind of a farm environment. I worked mowing and baling hay. I could handle a tractor and all that kind of stuff. After lunch we'd stretch out on the ground and take a nap. My dad and I just thoroughly enjoyed that relationship."

His father's influence has proven especially pivotal in the shaping of Ken's life in one important regard. He remembers his dad saying, "If I'm paying for you to go to medical school to do nothing but give shots, I'm wasting my money. What I want you to learn is the practice of preventive medicine."

The love and strong direction Ken's parents gave him as a child put a solid foundation under him. And today he sees many parallels between healthy family living and physical fitness. Both require consistent work and commitment. Relationships, like fitness, aren't static, he notes. If they aren't being regularly exercised and nourished, they are atrophying just like a muscle when it's unused.

"There's no way I can keep my body in shape unless I practice at least three, preferably four or five times a week," Ken points out. "Family relationships are exactly the same. You can't store them. Like exercise, they're an ongoing type of thing.

*I*n aerobic conditioning, we say it's got to be at least thirty minutes, three times a week. And it can't be just a blasé thirty minutes, it's got to be a good thirty minutes. You must get the heart rate up. The same is true in the family. Thirty minutes, three times a week, in strictly one hundred percent family communication and family relationship, and you experience a wonderful growth in the family's strength and health."

Family activities in the Cooper household center around travel and sports. And while every family member is interested in fitness, running has in particular met a special need in his daughter's life.

Berkeley has struggled with a learning disability which makes it especially hard for her to retain certain types of information. Academics are accomplished only with great difficulty and after much tutoring and help from specialists as well as from Dad and Mom. But when it comes to running, she is superb. And Ken is her number-one fan. He has spent hours encouraging her, timing her laps, running with her, and offering training tips.

"I've rushed home from speaking events and gone directly from the airport to the track meet so I could see her run," Ken says. "It's hard to beat being there and seeing my daughter come in first. It's just a thrill beyond words when she gets to the last lap of the two-mile run. To see her explode on that last lap and come in two hundred yards ahead—that's been one of my most satisfying experiences with my daughter."

Among his most memorable moments with Tyler have been hours and hours at his soccer matches and recently a five-day fishing trip they shared in Canada. Ken tore those five days out of his schedule and set them aside totally for Tyler. He finds it difficult to put into words the joy he felt watching his son pull in his first big northern pike. "It was an expensive trip," Ken says, "but worth every penny of it. I'll guarantee, even if I had to borrow the money to do it again, I would!"

Fathers who shoulder a lot of job responsibilities know all too well what Ken experiences—most of the demands placed on his schedule are not self-imposed requirements at that moment. Often the man becomes everyone's servant with no real control of his own time.

Ken reflects on a week in Colorado when he had promised he would spend his time exclusively with the family. In his briefcase was an unfinished manuscript his publisher was screaming for, an article he was writing for *Glamour* magazine, and an incomplete column for his newsletter. The briefcase tempted him all week. "But I didn't touch it," Ken says. "That was one of the hardest things I've done in a long time."

Ken Cooper's life-style can easily strain a marriage. And Ken admits that in the early years of his relationship with Millie, he didn't understand the importance of not letting his accomplishments overshadow hers. "If you bring your wife along with you as your career develops, and help her build her own identity, it just creates a harmonious situation that would otherwise be impossible," Ken wisely counsels.

Really, a wife is a partner, a helpmate; she's not just someone you marry to do the housework at home. A successful marriage takes a lot of work, a lot of nurturing, understanding, and compassion. So many couples," Ken observes, "go their own ways. He goes the golf route. He goes the hunting route with the boys. He plays cards. She goes the social route. They just get further and further apart."

Ken believes it takes a strong Christian foundation to keep a marriage relationship moving through the inevitable strains. "Whether it is uphill, downhill, or life on the flats, you have to have that foundation to work with from the beginning to provide a strong, running head start."

Will Ken's children bear any scars from his notoriety and the pressure from his work? "I don't think so," Ken responds. "I think Tyler will enjoy it. He calls himself the greatest; he's 'number one.' He has a real ego."

Ken remembers receiving a call one day in 1982 from the London Times, informing him that he was included in their list of seventy-four "greatest" people who had accomplished the most for mankind in the past twenty years. Ken was selected for contributing the most in the field of exercise and preventive medicine.

While it was quite an honor, the family wasn't overly impressed. "Do we get to go to England?" Millie asked. Her tongue-in-cheek comment served once again to keep Ken humble. And the only advantage he could gain in telling Tyler about it was being able to say, "Now you're not the greatest. Dad is!"

Ken Cooper's accomplishments have been phenomenal, a fact which he quickly and consistently credits to God's divine working. In college Ken thought he was headed into the Christian ministry, probably as a medical missionary. It was never his goal to acquire fame or wealth. In retrospect, he realizes his aerobics career has provided a far greater platform for sharing his Christian convictions than he would have had through ordinary ministry channels.

But Kenneth H. Cooper, M.D., is still working on his greatest task in life—being an effective father. "I'm trying to forge ahead into a new dimension, a new state in my life which is going to be a whole lot more family oriented than it has been in the past. I now realize that you don't gain back the tenth year from that child. You'll never have that year again. It's there only once in your life. If you don't use it now, it's lost forever."

BILL GAITHER

I *think when you set your priorities and say, 'not even the President is going to take me away from this priority,' you will have time to be a father. And if you do not, good things will just keep eating away at your effectiveness and family life.*

43

BILL GAITHER
Bill Gaither cherishes time with his family, limiting his days on the road to be with his children.

Music . . . and worship—four solid days of it—attract more than ten thousand friends and fans of The Bill Gaither Trio to Indianapolis's Convention Center every October for their annual Praise Gathering. The event—the largest of its kind—symbolizes both the popularity and the leadership in contemporary worship music Bill Gaither's trio has been providing for God's people for more than fifteen years.

Two Grammy Awards, one in 1973 for "Let's Just Praise the Lord" and the other in 1975 for "Jesus, We Just Want to Thank You," top the numerous accolades listed in the Trio's press kit. With more than two dozen LP album releases to their credit, combined sales long ago surpassed the million mark. And Bill Gaither has penned more than four hundred songs.

But children and family life are the top priorities in this singer-songwriter's life. Bill and his wife, Gloria (an accomplished song lyricist and the Trio's female vocalist), agree—the limits they have placed on the frequency and length of their concert tours and their career development have allowed their family life to prosper. And their three children, Suzanne, Amy, and Benjy, offer living testimony to a consistent pattern of parental concern.

Bill Gaither's passion for responsible living traces noticeably to roots in the Indiana farm life of his childhood. He was in sixth grade when he and his brother were handed the demanding assignment of milking the cows. It was an everyday and every night routine. And if done carelessly, leaving milk in the cow's udder, mastitis (a disease that ruins a cow for milk production) easily follows. So early on, Bill Gaither learned the disciplines of structure and hard work.

Today, those habits enhance his personal effectiveness and business management savvy. Bill is president of Alexandria House, his well-regarded music publishing company. And he serves education—his pre-trio career and the continuing love of both him and

Gloria—as a member of the board of directors for his alma mater, Anderson College.

With a frequency that embarrasses him, peers in the music business and promising young musicians alike look to Bill Gaither as a valued model, counselor, and friend. And to them this man, intent on succeeding first at home, truly is all those things.

The voice on the phone inquired, "Bill, do you have April seventh open?" He replied, "No, I'm booked at home that night." The caller continued, "Well, President Gerald Ford [then in office] is going to appear at the Grand Rapids Civic Center, and they want you to do the music." Bill Gaither paused, and then offered his response: "No, I've scheduled that night with the family."

Invitations to sing for the President aren't an everyday experience for this father of junior high, high school, and college-age children. "I still can't say on my press kit that I have sung before a president or a king or queen or any 'biggie.' So maybe I should have accepted," Bill Gaither reflects. But shunning even the slightest hint of a "superspiritual" attitude, he presses the point:

"It would be easy if all decisions were a choice between something good and bad. Certainly there was nothing bad about singing for the President. And I would not put anyone down for making the opposite choice. But in my situation, I had already been out the weekend before—Thursday, Friday, and Saturday—and I got in on Sunday and went to church. It would have meant leaving again on Monday night and being away from the kids another day and a half.

"I think when you set your priorities and say, 'not even the President is going to take me away from this priority,' you will have time to be a father. And if you do not, good things will just keep eating away at your effectiveness and family life." Bill Gaither works hard at consistently living out this perspective.

As the writer of over four hundred songs, president of Alexandria House (his music publishing company), and leader of the highly acclaimed Bill Gaither Trio, he never lacks for good causes clamoring for attention. In fact, keeping his schedule reined in is a never-ending effort. "Within the Christian field," he says, "you not only get requests; they come packaged in spiritual wrappings labeled 'God's will.' Well, it's only God's will for my life if I pray about it, think it through, and conclude it's God's will for my life."

Music in Bill's childhood home was enjoyed as a hobby, but no one ever thought of music as a worthy vocation. Bill's dad was a tool and die maker. They lived in central Indiana where all the relatives worked for General Motors in Anderson. The prevailing notion was that for a young man to make something of himself, he should acquire an early interest in math and work in engineering.

As a college English major, Bill prepared for a teaching career. It didn't occur to him that his lifelong fascination with music would lead to his resigning his high school teaching job to give music his full attention. But later, as he linked his talent with Gloria's musical gifts and with increasingly frequent church performances, that is what happened.

Eventually the growing popularity and success of the Bill Gaither Trio forced some tough choices. "For the sake of the family, we had to decide to go on the road only so many days each year." For the last twelve or thirteen years the Trio's concert tours have been limited to about two weeks each spring and fall. And Bill knows touring is vital to keeping one's perspective. "You get to meet real live flesh and blood people," he quips with more than tongue in cheek. "If you stayed in the studio all the time, you would start talking to yourself."

*B*ack home, the rest of the year is filled with writing, recording, and numerous other pressures which compete daily with the time it takes to be a caring parent. Bill knows, "Anything good takes time. There's no way around it. We fathers are kidding ourselves if we think it's not the quantity of time, but the quality. It's both. I'm not saying we have to be with our children day and night, but we do have to spend enough time so that we have as much impact as the other people who influence their lives."

This perspective resonates with Bill's early recollections of time with his own father. His dad was a "quietly directive" man who worked the swing shift from 3:00 p.m. to 11:00 p.m. During the school year that meant he was off to work by the time Bill and his brother and sister got home. But during the summer, Dad worked mornings and early afternoons on the family's fifty-acre farm. Bill was his willing helper.

Bill reminisces, "I was in the field every day with my dad doing something. The biggest thing I learned from him was the joy of working. We come from a hardworking family. I can remember days when we used to harvest and thresh wheat. The big extended family would come in—twenty-five, thirty, thirty-five people. . . ."

Though never lacking for love, Bill's was not an openly affectionate family. Love was expressed quietly. It's a style Bill still finds personally attractive. "I'm not against hugging," he cautions.

"We fathers are kidding ourselves if we think it's not the quantity of time, but the quality. It's both."

"With my own kids we are huggers and often verbalize our love. But I tend to trust over a long period of time those who are not so up front with their affections and feelings—who don't come on so strong."

The work ethic also expressed in Bill's childhood home was part and parcel of the prevailing philosophy that the best should be made of life, no matter what the circumstances. "The word *boring* was not allowed," Bill remembers. "It was dumb to get bored doing anything. You create your own excitement and your own joy out of the regularness of everyday life." That notion still ranks high on Bill's list of essential values. For the Gaithers, flashes in the pan are out, and long attention spans are definitely in.

Bill and Gloria stress at home that each person should develop and use his or her God-given talents as thoroughly as possible. "I'm a little bit tough on myself and Gloria and all our children in that I believe God put us here with certain resources, certain gifts and talents. We must be good stewards of those."

And with this discipline and emphasis upon using talents to the fullest often comes conflict. To get the best out of their songwriting, Bill and Gloria must often express criticism of the other's work.

"It's one thing," comments Bill, "to tell some lyricist, 'I don't think this is new. I don't think it's good enough. It's not fresh. We've said that before.' It's an entirely different thing to say that to Gloria, the person I love very dearly, the one with whom I share my deepest feelings. Sometimes it is tough. Sometimes it is very teary. But it's important to me that Suzanne, Amy, and Benjy, growing up in our home, see creative, talented people confronting and working things out and contributing mutually to the ministry.

The fact that one of the parties in these debates is a woman, holding her own in the creative process—that's especially important for Suzanne and Amy to see (and Benjy, too). They're two bright gals, and I don't want to see their talents and abilities put down simply because they're female."

Finding positive, Christlike ways to confront others is a high priority for Bill. "I want my kids to see how intelligent, loving people do it." Confrontation, he believes, "has something to do with making relationships very strong. We say that Jesus was gentle, meek, and mild. He was all those things. But he confronted people every day of his existence."

Benjy, Bill's youngest, has a bit of his father's explosive temper that has to be positively channeled. It concerns Bill. He and Gloria sometimes specifically choose to work out their conflicts in the presence of the children to demonstrate the valuable lesson that differences can be resolved in a loving and honest fashion.

"If Benjy fails to grasp this, he'll go on forever thinking you can do it by force," Bill reflects. "He'll assume the stronger person always wins. And sooner or later he'll meet up with somebody stronger than he is. And if *that's* the way it truly works, then someday we're going to find that some country has more nuclear weapons than we do, and they're going to destroy us. We've got to find positive ways in loving, Christian homes to help kids learn how to successfully work through confrontation."

Similarly, Bill knows that parents can't make all the life decisions for their children, and he emphasizes giving kids a "decision-making kit" which contains not only answers, but a good process for making decisions. "As parents we can only share with them where we've come so far on our journey," he says. "I guess this is the reason I want our children to see my seamy side, too. I want them to realize their dad isn't a perfect human being, just one who has special talents in some areas, and who works hard every day trying to hammer out God's will for his life."

If you assume from all this that *honesty* is highly prized in the Gaither home, you are right. To Bill it is extremely important that he and Gloria exemplify the kind of integrity that abhors not just cheating on income tax, but lying in any form.

"I've gone through some experiences in the Christian community in the last two or three years that have frustrated me," Bill says. "I'm hearing the words 'miscommunication,' 'misunderstood,' and 'a style problem' used a lot. Around our house we call it 'lying.' It's tragic to see a grown person who professes to love the Lord with all his heart who continually insists on lying.

"If the kids tell me they want to hurry home in order to do their homework, when the real reason happens to be to see a boyfriend, I try to stop them in their tracks and say, 'You don't have to lie about it. If seeing a friend is the real reason, then say so, and we can work with that. But we cannot deal with being untruthful.' "

*T*heir strategy for overcoming the tendency of every child to shade the truth is working. "Now, even Benjy, when I confront him with a real tough situation will say, 'Yes, I did that,' because he realizes that in the long run it's going to help him become the kind of person he wants to be."

Along with honesty, Bill Gaither stresses exploring *ideas* as a family. Ideas change the world, and Bill wishes every father would "get into the ideas business." He and Gloria model this by conversing regularly about politics and various social programs and issues. Family discussions often naturally tackle the implications of decisions made by the president, Congress, or the Supreme Court. "Kids are theological characters," Bill observes. "We've had a lot of good times with ideas, and we've had a lot of good times with our kids' friends in those discussions, too."

This exchange of ideas gives Bill insight into the natures of his own kids and how they are developing as individuals. It makes him better able to catch the generally subtle signals indicating that important developments or changes are taking place in their thinking and personalities.

"Kids are fragile and very complicated," he warns. "They all have different kinds of needs. You'd better have your ear pretty much to the ground. If you don't, I can see how kids develop resentful attitudes toward parents. Understanding kids is not as simplistic as I think a lot of Christian teachers would like to believe."

Another word not taken lightly by Bill Gaither is *relationship*. It's the substance of powerful human ties. And Bill recalls how the relationship formed with Suzanne, his firstborn. "After she was around for a while, I felt I might qualify to be a father. I didn't look at her right away with all kinds of ecstasy and deeply charged emotions. I've never been the kind of person to whom little kids come and want to jump up on my lap. When they get old enough to relate to on a cerebral level I do better.

"But, birth is a wonder. And with Suzanne . . . after nineteen years, I'm so tied into that kid in so many different kinds of emotional and intellectual and spiritual ways that I think it would take all the forces of hell itself to separate us. This only happens when we totally understand what *relationship* means."

The understandings and ties that come from caring time with his children consistently help Bill Gaither grasp their changing needs. "Traditionally we have left this to the wife." But Bill believes, "We fathers need to develop a good sensitive mechanism that can warn us early to do some preventive maintenance. Too many fathers are insensitive to such signals, only to find themselves later saying, 'I wish I'd done this . . . I wish I'd done that. . . .' " Bill wonders, "For how many more generations are we going to keep saying it?"

There are no easy answers to hard problems. That was the message in some sermons which had an impact on Bill's thinking. A fun, realistic, and vigorous view of homelife is the path which has been chosen by this "fellow struggler" in the high call of being an effective father.

STAN SMITH

*Living up to one's
ideals is difficult. I fight the
temptation to become
comfortable with the relatively
easy life readily possible in
our society. I want to help my
kids, as young as they are,
to learn this.*

55

STAN SMITH
Though the Smith family enjoys sports, Stan wants his kids to develop their own abilities, whatever those may be.

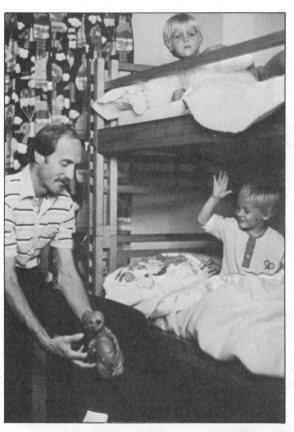

What is it like to be the best tennis player in the world? Stan Smith knows—twice over. In both 1972 and 1973, the International Tennis Federation named him number one in the world—the zenith of a dazzling pro career that has filled several trophy cases with the glint of gold and silver.

At Forest Hills in 1971, he won the United States Open singles competition and a year later took the singles title at Wimbledon. For eleven years straight, Stan played on the Davis Cup team, and he was rated the top male singles player in America in 1969, 1971, 1972, and 1973.

As a boy growing up in Pasadena, California, Stan quickly showed promise as an all-around athlete. Although adept at high school basketball and football, a local tennis clinic coach encouraged him to specialize in tennis. It was good advice, for despite a relatively late start in the game, he quickly advanced through amateur ranks while a student at the University of Southern California. He turned pro in 1968.

Stan now lives near Hilton Head, South Carolina, with his wife, Margie, two sons, Ramsey and Trevor, and a daughter, Logan. He writes instructional articles for *Tennis* magazine and makes frequent promotional appearances on behalf of Adidas shoes and clothing, Fischer racquets, and the Hilton Head Resort. He finds time each year to instruct at a few tennis camps and manage his business affairs. Stan also remains active on the pro tennis circuit, and in 1984 reached the finals in the Over Thirty-Five Division of the U.S. Open Tennis Tournament.

*A*s a six-foot, four-inch, 180-pound tennis player, Stan Smith seems to collect oversize adjectives. Sportswriters speak of his "mighty power" and "courageous solidity." His eyes are the blue of "still waters that run deep" and his nose "meanders down his face like an Allegheny ridge."

This giant of a man packs self-discipline and purposefulness on an enormous scale. In the words of one Davis Cup teammate, Smith has a "great inner calm about him—I think he has the most integrity of any man in sports."

It's no surprise, then, to discover that Stan Smith also holds bedrock convictions about fatherhood. As dad to two young sons, Ramsey and Trevor, and a daughter, Logan, Stan approaches parenting with the same thoughtful persistence with which he plays tennis.

Stan thought a lot about the importance of the family even before he and his wife Margie had their first child. Stan recalls, as a youngster, noticing the significance of the family unit. "It seems clear to me that any successful society was so because of its strong families. And the downfall of every unsuccessful society began when its families started to fail. I feel strongly that my family must take priority in my life."

This understanding of the importance of the family was fostered by the home in which Stan grew up. Stan's dad, a college coach and later a real estate agent, epitomized the quiet, successful, hardworking man who provided well for his family and commanded their respect in return. He was a tough disciplinarian who insisted his three sons help with regular chores around the house.

Neither his father nor mother pushed Stan along in tennis. If they had, rebellion may well have surfaced. At least that's what torpedoed the six years of piano lessons Stan took—including a summer music camp in the Colorado Rockies when he was twelve. Nowadays he doesn't play the piano at all.

Stan's folks began to actively follow his tennis when he was in college. The first time he played the Davis Cup tournament in Australia, they saved up to be there. Supporting Stan's tennis career has since become a major focus of his father's fifteen years of retirement.

Does a family heritage like this make it easier for Stan to mix world-class tennis with successful family living? Like any father, Stan faces daily the challenge in one or more of its subtle variations. But for Stan, the inevitable conflicts of time and commitment have thus far not become a major problem.

There is one vital ingredient in Stan's life often missing in the lives of many others—perspective. Long ago he realized that tennis, while a great means, could never be an adequate end for living. So simple a question as, "What happens if I break my leg and can't play again?" proves his point.

The quest for a truly adequate life philosophy haunted Stan during his sophomore year at the University of Southern California. He began to carefully watch friends whose lives seemed to exhibit true substance. And he asked a lot of questions about the sources of that meaning. Through a book, a friend introduced him to athletes who had committed their lives to Jesus Christ.

*I*t began to dawn on Stan that regular church attendance—his custom for years until Sundays became dominated by tennis tournaments—wasn't enough. Stan reappraised his Christianity. Then one night, after several weeks of soul-searching, Stan quietly admitted his personal need and resubmitted to the Lordship of Christ.

This sparked a reordering of his life priorities. Stan's demanding travel schedule was one of the areas he questioned. For many traveling fathers, family life is a choppy sea of traumatic farewells, long-distance phone calls, and all-too-short reunions. Stan has managed to balance the priorities of tennis and family by taking his young family with him on the circuit.

"It's worked out very well," he says. "It hasn't been as easy as traveling alone, but it hasn't been as tough traveling with young children as people think. Obviously it's more difficult financially, but we've been able to handle that. And it's been terrific that I get to spend a great deal of time with my kids."

As a family on the tour, Stan suspects he has actually been able to give his kids more time than most fathers do. He has worked aggressively at being there—participating in the ebb and flow of day-to-day parenting and consciously avoiding the familiar "absentee father" trap.

It helps that Margie is at home in the world of tennis. She first met Stan when he was seventeen and had just won the U.S. National Junior Championships. She was twelve and "ball boy" at one of his matches. Sometime later he saw her again at a tournament and autographed the cast on her broken arm.

*T*hey met again while Stan was in college. Margie was then eighteen and ranked fifth nationally among junior women players. During her junior and senior college years the relationship turned serious. They were married in 1974.

"Often I see in families a husband who, at the office, makes all the major decisions," Stan says. "He returns to a home where his wife is the major decision maker. There's no equal sharing of responsibilities. The husband says, 'Do whatever you want to do,' and the effect is often disastrous." Stan believes it's essential that his children see him sharing leadership responsibilities at home. And he's the first to admit that staying involved in the decision-making process isn't easy.

"Sometimes I expend so much energy on the tennis court, I just don't want to get involved in those decisions. That's when it requires special effort." That's also when the seeds of self-discipline planted by his own father, and watered by countless hours of persistence on the tennis court, blossom into a Smith family strength.

To Stan's way of thinking, self-control is central. The character quality of persistence that his children must ultimately possess turns on that pivot. And Stan is determined that his kids will learn that personal growth is never an easy carousel ride. Rather, self-discipline develops by facing life's challenges and difficulties.

George Toley, Stan's coach for many years, recalls Stan's exceptional persistence. During an NCAA match, Stan seemed sluggish—simply not on his game. Toley was appalled. After the match he berated Stan for a full fifteen minutes. Stan listened quietly to every word and then softly mentioned that during the first set he had sprained his ankle. He had played out the match without complaint.

"I stress working hard and getting the most out of the time you have," says Stan. "I emphasize that it's not going to be easy, that you have to be able to tough it out in all sorts of situations. Living up to one's ideals is difficult, much like the challenge of becoming the best player in the world. I try to live out these goals—to fight the temptation to become comfortable with the relatively easy life readily possible in our society. I want to help my kids, as young as they are, to learn this."

For Ramsey this translates into daily assignments like emptying the trash, making his bed, and keeping his room tidy. It also means exercising the self-control and good manners often difficult for a young lad, but expected of him by Dad.

While Stan Smith's public example as an outstanding athlete measures up to these ideas, he is quick to point out the downside—in a close family, members also see each other at their worst. "My kids observe me in almost every situation," he says. "On the court, I think Ramsey understands the competitiveness of the situation. If I act like a jerk, I can't expect him to act differently. A parent must be able to bring his child to the tennis match or into any other situation and not be embarrassed. If it's truly comfortable to have them there, then the code of behavior is being lived out with integrity."

Stan is also aware that his success in athletics, and the esteem in which our society holds athletes, can easily become a hard act for his kids to follow. He's concerned that his success not overwhelm or discourage them. He doesn't want his kids to be subtly tricked into thinking their self-worth can be found in trying to imitate or surpass their father's fame.

"When my kids ask me tough questions about sex or other important issues, I want to be able to respond easily, honestly, and without embarrassment."

"The pressure, whether external or internal, to be an overachiever can ruin a family," says Stan. "I want my kids to live with balance and do their best in life at whatever they tackle."

A particular personality trait can often help in one area of life and hinder in another. It is no different for Stan Smith. He is famous for his coolness on the court. Vic Braden, one of the foremost tennis teaching professionals says, "Stan is a lot like Jack Kramer in his ability to put all external stimuli aside on the court. He does not permit himself to get involved in emotional issues out here." During the 1971 U.S. Open, many players complained about the court ban on racket throwing and abusive language. In the midst of it all, said *Time* magazine, "Smith went serenely on his way, demolishing everyone he met." This emotional coolness aids his concentration in tennis, but it is one of his greatest barriers to being an effective husband and father.

"I don't communicate well in general," Stan admits. "I'm nervous about it. I want to be the sort of parent who is ready and able to communicate easily about the tough problems my children run into. I really hope they'll feel an openness and freedom to discuss those problems with me. So I work at it. One day when my kids ask me the tough questions about sex or other important issues, I want to be able to respond easily, honestly, and without embarrassment. It's up to me to help my son or daughter feel he or she can freely talk with me about anything."

Stan understands the power of nonverbal communication as well. He believes it is the strength of his own marriage that will most strongly shape the expectations his kids form for their own. "I try to be openly affectionate around Margie and the kids, to demonstrate that touching is important. I frequently say, 'I love you.' While certainly a well-worn phrase, those three words cannot be heard too often in a family. If my sons and daughter see this modeled as they grow up, I'm confident they will be able in turn to communicate with me, with their friends, and eventually with their future spouses. Communication is my weak point, so I continually work at it with the kids and with Margie."

How does Stan Smith show this affection and interest? "You demonstrate it by being attentive and by being there as much of the time as you can." When his kids ask Stan a question, he responds right away so they won't end up repeating it several times to be heard. Stan's reply may be, "Please wait until I'm finished." The important point is that he shows them respect by responding quickly and receives their respect in return.

Stan and Margie handle parenting much like doubles players— trading off to afford the other time to be alone or to work individually with each of the children. The whole Smith family spends many hours out-of-doors, sometimes swimming together or perhaps kicking a ball around.

Stan is convinced that giving his kids recognition and respect is crucial. He is a hands-on kind of father, and that includes helping out when diapers need changing. Twice or more a week whether he's at home or with the boys on the road, he reads to them at bedtime. "It always opens up special opportunities for questions and communication," comments Stan. *ValueTales*, a series of children's books about famous people, is Ramsey's current favorite. He can quote many of the lines as he's learning about the inventiveness of Edison or the curiosity of Columbus.

Of course, no man fathers with perfection. And with years to go before Stan can measure the true fruit of his labors, he avoids any suggestion that he has fathering aced. But Stan Smith approaches his daily fathering assignment with the kind of reason, intensity, humility, joy, and laughter that makes him a delight to hug and call "Dad."

NOEL STOOKEY

We understand the paradox of discipline and freedom—that you're not doing a child a service in giving him no limits. If you show him what the restrictions are, he will find ways to fly absolutely free within those limits.

NOEL STOOKEY
South Blue Hill, Maine, with its winter population of 1500, is a perfect setting for the laid-back family life Noel Stookey prefers.

The fresh sounds of Peter, Paul, and Mary's first album can raise goose bumps on your arms today as quickly as they did in 1961. The protest years of Vietnam and civil rights were just beginning. Students were shedding lackadaisical attitudes in favor of earthshaking confrontation, and PP&M music quickly became the potent statement of an earnest generation's left-of-center politics.

Remarkably, the warmth, simplicity, and power of the trio remains untarnished by today's trendy world of popular music. Maybe it's their synergy—the effect was always more than the simple sum of the trio's parts. Those who enjoy the group in concert are surprised when Paul Stookey (the tall one with the scholarly stoop) ably doubles as a human sound effects machine. From creaking doors to loose bands on a suburbanite's transmission, he creates whatever audio support his humorous monologues require.

And anyone given to reading record labels also quickly recognizes Noel Paul Stookey as the superb songwriter of such favorites as "The Wedding Song," "I Dig Rock and Roll Music," and (with Peter Yarrow) "One Kind Favor."

Collectors prize the numerous Peter, Paul, and Mary albums, but Noel has since added to his credits several solo LPs including "Paul And" (1971), "One Night Stand" (1972), "Something New and Fresh" (1978), "Band and Bodyworks" (1979), and, most recently, "State of the Heart" (1984).

Late in 1968, Noel Stookey quietly chose to turn his back on the endless plane tickets, hotel rooms, and isolation of on-the-road stardom. He could no longer ignore the lengthening shadow of discontent betraying the reality behind his well-groomed public image.

At the urging of a friend, Bob Dylan, Noel turned with a hungry heart to search again the Bible. And the arrows of God's truth found their mark. John Henry Bosworth, better known as Noel Paul Stookey, did the unthinkable for a sixties activist. He became a Christian.

Desiring a solitude New York's suburbs couldn't deliver and the opportunity for his children to experience the qualities of rural life he had known in Maryland and the Midwest, Noel moved the family—first to the banks of a small pond in Westchester, New York, and then to the brusque beauty of Maine's coast at South Blue Hill. There he settled with Betty, his wife of twenty-one years, and daughters Elizabeth, Katherine, and Anna. There he reclaimed a four-story hen house for a recording studio. And there he continued rediscovering not only himself, but his family.

Today Noel divides his time and undiminished talents between fathering and his better-known but not more important specialties of songwriting, performing, and producing.

Acoustic guitars in hand, few musicians in the turbulent sixties enjoyed louder applause or a more affectionate following than the trio of Peter, Paul, and Mary. Millions knew Paul Stookey's voice, his skill as a guitarist, his wit, his self-assured image, and his stylish sense of taste.

"I felt as if my life were straight out of the amusement park scene in *Pinocchio*," Stookey once reflected. "I traveled first class. I had limos waiting for me at the airport. I was protected. It's very strange to be in the marketplace with yourself, rather than with a product. The product becomes you. And if someone says, 'You're so genuine,' it becomes: 'Step right up and get your genuineness.'

"I had built this apparatus that had the face of Noel, whose arms and legs moved and went through all the right motions, but somewhere inside of me there was a little boy who wanted to be closer to what it was that made him happy. And he wasn't finding it in this image."

So in 1968, Noel Paul Stookey headed for home—a destination characterized by much more than familiar front steps, doorposts, and a bed that instinctively knew how to cradle his lanky frame. Going home this time meant the reassessing of priorities and striking a kind of unstructured pace in life which supports, indeed forces, soul-cleansing encounters with reality.

In the preceding couple of years, Noel Stookey's spiritual journey had been undergoing the quiet revolutions of a personal encounter with God. And his new commitment to Jesus Christ renewed his commitment to his family—the environment where he thought his conversion should most be evidenced. "Two hundred days on the road does not make for a good family life," he says. "I decided that the only way I was going to get a handle on what was important was to stop." He told Peter and Mary he wouldn't tour anymore.

*P*reviously, Betty, his high school friend and bride of twenty-one years, had functioned virtually as a single parent to their daughter Elizabeth. (The twins, Katherine and Anna, who quickly altered Betty's capacity to handle family life without Noel's regular help, didn't arrive until 1971.) There was tension and adjustment needed as Noel's strong pendulum swing moved him well into her home territory. But after playing for a while what he describes as the "zealous convert" role, he realized that to drop music altogether was also not the answer. If handled properly, both family and professional responsibilities could be nourished at the same time.

"Even in the family, it could be understood that Dad writes songs, that he has a talent for making people come together, for

71

expressing things. So in 1972, I started traveling again." And for Betty, it was a relief to discover that Noel's newfound balance held. Her husband's love for Peter, Paul, and Mary, now replaced by a passion for God, wasn't going to erode their family life again.

Several years later, this balance finds the Stookey family together more than two-thirds of the time and very much in love with life in the small, rural community of South Blue Hill, Maine—winter population of 1,500. Their homelife vividly reflects much of the warmth and support Noel received growing up as an only child. He recalls the advantages and disadvantages.

"The advantages were that there certainly was no lack of attention. Every question that I didn't feel embarrassed about bringing up was answered. I'd say, 'Mom, what does this mean?' And there would be a blackboard and piece of chalk—as well as the extra time she wouldn't have had if I had brothers and sisters."

Noel's dad, a district sales manager for a rubber company, was a gregarious man, loved by every neighborhood kid. And he had an affection for music, evidenced by the four-string tenor guitar he kept around the house. He also had played drums in a dance band he led while growing up in Utah. Young Noel Stookey began to experiment with music and comedy, and his dad encouraged him.

"He would come in through the door from a hard day of work and see that I hadn't mowed the lawn like I was supposed to, and he'd say 'Noel!' And I'd say, 'Yeah, Dad, down in the basement.' He'd come down in the basement and I'd have a tape recorder and microphone spread all over the floor. And I'd say, 'Dad, come here. Put on these earphones. Listen to this!' And I'd been spending an hour working on sound effects when I should have been doing the lawn. Finally he'd just crack up, just melt, and then I'd get the lawn done. But it hadn't been done when he wanted it done. He was accessible."

"Two hundred days on the road does not make for a good family life. The only way I was going to get a handle on what was important was to stop."

The lack of blunt, down-to-earth, and sometimes biting feedback of the kind only brothers and sisters can dish out is a major

72

disadvantage to being an only child, Noel recalls.

"If as a child I presumed or postured something I wasn't, and if I'd had a brother or sister, he'd have hit me in the arm or she'd have stepped on my toe and said, 'Come on, get off it!' I didn't really experience that until my early thirties, and that's a long time to go through life having concealments and walls because you thought some things were better hidden from other people."

As a father, Noel has sought to craft a homelife that offers his daughters the best of both worlds. Love, a belief in the importance of the family, and a deeply ingrained sense of fun are the building blocks of the Stookeys' family success. Their warmth can be traced to Noel's penchant for clowning and teasing—strong reflections of the optimism and sense of spontaneity translated from his own childhood family experience.

"I'm an incorrigible father in terms of loving to get a response from my kids," he says. "I certainly do cultivate spontaneity with them. I like to break down what I see as social barriers."

This sense of laughter and celebration invades even the devotional aspects of their family life. They're willing to depart from convention. Dinner table grace, for example, can become one of the most interactive times of their day.

"I love to say off-the-wall graces," Noel admits. "We take turns. They may not be brief. They deal with the problems or joys of the day. They sometimes ask for strength. They express what I pray is the individual response to God's calling in each of my children's lives. God has dealt with me very individually. His gentleness has encouraged me to write about him. And so, because that rings so true in my life and talent, I feel that's what I must bring to my family. I don't mind being the spokesman.

"The thing that has emerged most predominant in our prayers for these last three or four months has been thanking God for the hardships, for the tests, for the ability to develop strengths, knowing that he loves us, that he is there."

Noel recognizes that each family member must develop a personal prayer relationship with God. So prayers at night are left to each child. "There are times when we'll pray together at night, but there are many times when I'll say, 'Don't forget to mention that in your prayers.' "

Noel believes the quality of relationship within a family is clearly a reflection of the strength or weakness of the parents' marital bond.

A weak marriage will detract from the quality of time spent with children. Problems elsewhere in a father's life will distract him from healthily concentrating on the kids. "There'll be a certain driven aspect to your relationship," he asserts.

Consequently, Noel knows that he and Betty must be careful to allow time together. They keep at it. "I'm fortunate to have a wife I went to high school with," he says. "But it's not just the length of time married, sometimes it's the cultural background. We are fortunate to share many attitudes about children."

One of those common perspectives is the importance of guidelines in a child's life. It's reflected in Noel's and Betty's care to avoid going two different ways at once, thereby frustrating themselves and confusing their kids.

"We understand the paradox of discipline and freedom—that you're not doing a child a service in giving him no limits. If you show him what the restrictions are, he will find ways to fly absolutely free within those limits. We are concerned for his well-being. That is why we impose those limits. Just as the petulant child smashes the window to gain attention, so we give attention of sorts by imposing certain limits."

*T*hese limits are well-decorated with love in the physically demonstrative atmosphere of the Stookey household. But surprisingly, Noel finds himself frustratingly awkward at expressing emotions in words.

"I can say so much more with a hug—it speaks volumes," he stresses. "But sometimes hugs are not sufficient. Sometimes words are necessary—emotional words—and those times I find the hardest to comply with."

Emphatic love like this has an all-important corrective function in parenting. Noel has faced the disconcerting experience of misreading his child's apparent motive in doing something wrong. "I've made the mistake of punishing a child for something she didn't do because, if it had been me, I would have done it," he says.

Because travel for performances and recording dates still takes Noel away from his family for about a hundred days a year, he sometimes employs special efforts on the road to keep in touch with the children. Using the mail is his favorite. The children never know what delights the postman may bring next—a short note or letter, a small stick-on compass, a Smurf, or a magazine clipping with mustaches drawn on the faces.

Writing is real important," asserts Noel. "Anybody can recall the thrill of receiving something in the mail. The telephone doesn't do it. The telephone is okay for Dad and Mom, because there are certain pertinent details that have to be taken care of right away. But the thrill of the postman bringing something for you from some exotic, faraway place—maybe even Cincinnati—can be an important event for a child when her father is on the road."

Fathering models as diverse as fellow PP&M member Peter Yarrow and the Old Testament patriarch Abraham have shaped Noel's views. Noel finds amazing the amount of time he observed Peter expending upon fathering. While on the road, he was on the phone every day reviewing his son's homework assignments.

Affectionately calling him "the driven Peter," Noel still shakes his head in wonder that Peter spent so much time and did so much in his role as a single parent.

The saga of Abraham and Isaac strikes in Noel so resonate a chord because it poignantly mixes the priorities of duty to God and duty toward one's children. Noel is especially taken by the way God spoke to Abraham as contrasted to his own experience with God.

I think about how God has spoken to me and realize that there is a boldness of action on Abraham's part that means one of three things: either I am living in a more tentative age or God spoke louder or Abraham listened harder. If I were called upon to take my child to the rock, God would have to speak very loudly. I assume, therefore, that God spoke very loudly to Abraham. Mankind was essentially the same then as it is now. To be called to perform such an act as a sign of faith took a strong calling. I really pray that I listen that well!"

And Noel's is no idle prayer. He has grappled deeply with the concern that he establish for his daughters both appropriate limits and significant opportunities for their individual gifts to flourish.

Interestingly, the quaint and profoundly simple but limited opportunities of life in South Blue Hill mirror the tension. The high school Noel and Betty attended as kids in Birmingham, Michigan, teemed with comprehensive extracurriculars—everything from hands-on journalism to auto shop to a radio broadcasting workshop that really taught how to put imagination into a radio script.

In Blue Hill, the local student body of less than four hundred automatically limits curriculum options. Even more significantly, Noel knows that each daughter must ultimately make up her own mind about holding on to the values of Blue Hill or tempering them with ideals from the "other world" of large houses, material things, and New York City high life.

This recognition has led Noel and Betty to provide Elizabeth the opportunity to attend prep school; there the challenges were better fitted to her capabilities and would open more doors for her future. The decision has turned out to be one of their wisest. Elizabeth has blossomed. Noel even suspects she is hiding poetic skills of Bob Dylan proportions if she ever decides to let them out.

The issues of roots and wings, of supplying the grist from which children can properly mill their own Christian faith are for Noel Stookey ideals of parenting not easily lived up to. He often falls short, but takes heart in another family fundamental—forgiveness.

"Children's expectations are much like God's," he thinks. "They love you just the way you are. If you want to improve, that's fine with them, too. But they would like you just the way you are."

GRAHAM KERR

More than time is required to heal a badly broken family. It takes meaningful actions and knowing how to say "I love you."

GRAHAM KERR
With two grown children and a teenager, these days
Graham is learning to cuddle grandchildren (lower right).

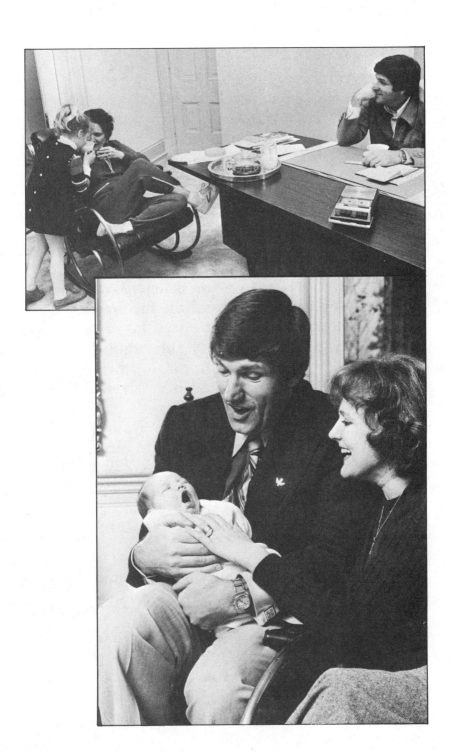

Americans love cowboys . . . and food. So when CBS invited Englishman Graham Kerr, astride his proven steed of rich recipes, to leap chairs in the kitchen of their New York television studios, "The Galloping Gourmet" consented. He was immediately a new American hero and off to another hit series.

At thirty-seven years of age, Graham Kerr was possibly the best known food authority in the world, and certainly the highest paid. "The Galloping Gourmet" was being translated into several languages and attracting consistent acclaim and awards around the world. This only child of a thoroughly English mother and predominantly Scottish father had achieved professional acclaim beyond even his wildest youthful yearnings.

Yet money, travel, privilege, and prestige proved insufficient substance for successful living. The rocketlike ascent of his career had left little time to grow as a person or to nourish his marriage to Treena or his relationship with their three children. "Treena turned to a variety of mood-changing drugs and alcohol," Graham recalls, "to withstand the pressures of producing my TV show and keeping up with my frantic life-style. I was a disaster as a father."

Notes posted on the refrigerator door had become too frequently the only communication with the children. The rigors of a smash daily television show found Graham and Treena returning home long after their live-in nurse had put the kids to bed.

It took more than his thirteen-year-old daughter Tessa's near fatal overdose of painkillers to bring Graham to his senses. It nearly took his life. "The Galloping Gourmet" series ended when he and Treena were almost killed in a violent highway accident while ambitiously touring the country with cameras and crews to make one hundred programs. Graham's left side was partially paralyzed, and the trauma left Treena unable to work at all.

"We gathered up our three children, licked our wounds, and retired with our small fortune to sail about the world," recounts Graham. "Our object was to recover our strength and see how the 'other half'—those who sat in *front* of the TV screen—lived." What they discovered would eventually change their eating habits, family relationships, life-style, and ultimately the whole focus of their lives.

The revolution dawned slowly and not without a good deal of trial and error, punctuated by the loss of part of their secure "fortune" when the corporation in which they had invested heavily went bankrupt. The changes took on their final significance when first Treena and then Graham became reborn as Christians.

Today the Kerrs, now grandparents, enjoy the restored love and respect of their children and preach a different and far more whole gospel. It's rooted in simplicity and their love of Jesus Christ, instead of hedonistic overconsumption. In 1978, they responded to a call to demonstrate to American Christians how simpler living could result in excess resources being made available to help the poor of the world feed themselves. Operation L.O.R.D. (Long-Range Development for the World) was established. Through its efforts in helping churches train their people, third-world families in places like Bella Horizonte, Brazil, and in other developing nations are feeding themselves from food they can harvest on their own carefully planned quarter-acre "farms."

Graham Kerr's roller coaster ride with food has returned to level ground, and he couldn't be more thrilled about where he has landed.

*I*n the early 1970s, Graham Kerr was the most popular and highest paid chef in the world. And to this day he remains fascinated with what food contributes to the quality of our lives. But cooking isn't Graham Kerr's greatest talent; it is only window dressing on his real gift. Graham is a dreamer, an entrepreneur, a visionary.

For his first forty years, his well-honed talents produced great fame and wealth, and an equal serving of grief and despair. Little could this bright, athletic lad from Sussex, England, have imagined the tangled web his choices would spin.

Raised in an English home, Graham remembers little about his life before age eleven, except for his appallingly low sense of self-worth. "I can't remember ever playing a single game with either of my parents, being hugged or hearing the simple words, 'I love you,' " he laments, "although I've been assured that I was loved." Graham's father was something of an amateur actor and earned a living for the family as a surveyor and architect for a London brewery.

Dad went away to war when Graham was five, not to return for three years. Graham was shipped off to boarding school and Mom went to work for a brief time with the Air Force. After Nazi Germany fell and John Kerr returned home, he and his wife decided upon a career change that would set the stage for the rest of Graham's life. They put their considerable administrative skills to work as hoteliers, managing some of England's finest hotels.

At age fourteen, Graham left the Rudolph Steiner Theosophy School and a sweet young lass who had caught his eye, to return "home"—now a hotel manager's suite. Hotel servants and the fascinating life-style of wealthy guests quickly replaced his thoughts of school chums.

Soon Graham decided he would follow in his father's footsteps, but not exactly. As a lad helping about the kitchen and dining room of the Roebuck Hotel in Wych Cross, England, he began to dream. He imagined so enhancing the image of food, wine, and service that he could rise above the "servant" image and gain peer acceptance by the upper class and the nouveau riche. It became a consuming ambition.

Although his mother was an excellent cook, Polish and French chefs provided Graham's early lessons. Climbing the ranks as a sixteen-year-old, he remembers the day the headwaiter commanded, "Time to try your hand at being a waiter, Master Graham." Nor will he ever forget the expression of Lord Harley Shawcross, his first customer and a man of impeccable manners. With a flourish, Graham served the gentleman's buttery Dover sole right onto the tablecloth where a plate should have been.

The embarrassment was not without purpose, however. It sparked in Graham a growing and critical recognition that social status was not only reflected in what people ate, but how they ate it. That insight would eventually make him "The Galloping Gourmet."

At age eighteen, Graham was drafted into the British army. As a catering adviser he had become a Second Lieutenant when, without his parents' enthusiastic approval, he married his boarding school sweetheart, Treena.

To their mutual surprise, Treena soon informed Graham that he was to become a father. "Tessa was born one year, one day, and one hour after the wedding," he reflects. "I was very excited and told everybody." The reality of three living on a single officer's salary, however, was less exciting. No "marriage allowance" would be available until he reached age twenty-three.

Graham's inability to recall any warm early childhood memories became in many ways Tessa's legacy, for he had little idea about how to form a relationship with his little girl. The failure was

"I can't remember ever playing a single game with either of my parents, being hugged, or hearing the simple words, 'I love you.' "

underscored when, years later, he discovered that at age fifteen she had penned in her diary a plot to kill him. At that time Graham's career was in high gear, and he had little patience for anything that competed with his pressured professional schedule.

While the chief catering adviser for the Royal New Zealand Air Force, Graham was approached by the New Zealand Broadcasting Corporation to host a radio foods show for women. Some scripts were approved, and by Christmas of 1959 the show was a growing success in spite of what its producer had initially called "the world's most boring voice."

At first Graham was a rather reluctant celebrity. "All of my cherished memories of food experiences were exhausted in the first series of nine-minute lectures," he recalls. "When they asked me to do another series my reply was 'Well . . . er . . . yes, I suppose so.'

"Conversely, all of my wildest dreams were coming true: People were listening to me talk about food and wine and interesting places, not as a cook, but as a radio personality. I really was 'somebody'! And I appreciated the ten dollars a program the hard work was generating."

Andy, very much a planned son, expanded the family while they lived in New Zealand. Eight years later another daughter, Kareena, was born. But family life became almost nonexistent as Treena's considerable creative talents were enlisted to produce Graham's television shows. They typically worked from late morning until midnight to produce the sixty-five shows devoured by a thirteen-week series. Twelve weeks of frantic preparation would follow for the next series—always including a world tour to gather new recipes. But spurred on by success, acclaim, and profits, the absurd pace continued for eight more years.

Family life went begging. The kids hated the notoriety. Tour buses passed by their substantial house, and too often the question was asked, "Aren't you 'The Galloping Gourmet's' daughter?" The climate was perfect for a textbook case of rebellion.

Graham and Treena hired the best live-in nurse they could find. But communication with the children became characterized by quickly scribbled notes left about the house for one another. Many things were acquired, which led to privileges offering access to the right people, but these were hollow achievements indeed.

"As the show, now on 260 stations, expanded," says Graham, "so did the tremendous hurt building in our lives. There was no time for reflection. And for a long time we ignored it." The Kerr family became 'Exhibit A' in the chapter on consumption in the manual on disposable life-styles. Emotional debts mounted. "Unwittingly," says Graham, "we were getting lost in the garbage ourselves."

Graham vividly recalls sitting in a theater with Treena in 1970 watching *Lawrence of Arabia*. "The manager, having recognized us as we entered, tapped me on the shoulder. We were wanted at the hospital. Tessa, then thirteen, was having her stomach pumped, because she had taken an overdose of painkillers. We were shocked. But she recovered and, unfortunately, so did we."

A violent accident on U.S. Highway 101 in April of 1971 finally brought the Kerrs' treadmill to a halt, and them back to their senses. They were asleep in a motor home on tour, taping a herculean one hundred TV shows, when a semitrailer truck struck them. They should have been killed. Fortunately, only the show died.

Collecting themselves and their considerable resources, the family set sail for the next two years on a seventy-foot ocean racing ketch. She had all the appointments, including the second prize in Lloyds of London's "Yacht of the Year" Award. The course they charted was supposed to heal their lives. But a half-million-dollar cruise along the coasts of England and America, as well as through the Mediterranean and the Caribbean, proved only that it takes more than time to heal a badly broken family. It takes actions and knowing how to say "I love you" and mean it.

One pivotal insight, however, did surface. Life aboard ship led to much simpler eating—meats, vegetables, and fresh fruit without sauces and marinades. The heavy feeling that rich foods and desserts had for years left in their stomachs vanished, and the entire family felt better. Graham and Treena became so accustomed to simple eating that following an anniversary dinner of rich French food, they both became sick to their stomachs in the middle of the night.

The yacht was traded for a twenty-four room mansion on the Chesapeake. The Kerr family returned to America, but not yet to their senses. Graham wanted to come back to his fans as their "custom designer of quality living." It was a brilliant piece of conceptual creativity, but the new TV show, titled "Take Care"—a pun on the pronunciation of Graham's last name—thrust them back into familiar and destructive routines. There was one exception: the simple diet continued. Rich foods now nauseated them. The complete transformation of Graham Kerr as a father and the healing of relationships with his children were slowly in the making.

A call from Graham's agent in February of 1975 provided the next curious piece of the puzzle. "A bishop who heard your speech last week wants you to do a tour of the United States speaking to his denomination," he said. "Willie, you must be joking," Graham responded. "I spoke about the poor people of the world and their great need for food while we overfeed ourselves in our obese culture. But preaching on poverty simply isn't my style." What was becoming increasingly obvious to Graham and Treena was the massive difference in their lives a seemingly simple commitment of themselves to the person of Jesus Christ was making.

Treena had become a Christian first, and the resulting inner contentment she was experiencing had become extremely attractive to Graham. One evening he returned to his hotel room after fourteen hours of television taping. He was very tired and very frustrated with his seeming inability to make contact with God.

Bible reading and eloquent prayers uttered self-consciously on his knees had failed him. "What do I have to say to you to get to know you like Treena?" Graham wondered aloud to God.

"Jesus, I love you," finally spilled from his lips, followed by a sudden and most wonderful sense of inner peace. "It was like the whole ceiling was rolled back by the hand of God," Graham recalls, "as Jesus reached down to me and loved *me* right back. A wonderful thrill ran right through me. I chatted and chatted and chatted to him about this and that and the other—we had our first talk together."

The broken relationships of Graham's life began to be restored. He and Treena discovered a unity in praying together they had never thought possible or experienced during all their years of working in close communication. Graham came to realize that a restored relationship with Tessa, Andy, and Kareena could not be

Graham realized that a restored relationship with his kids could not be demanded, no matter how badly he wanted it.

demanded, no matter how right it might be or how badly he wanted it. He would have to release them—set them free so that they could choose freely whether or not to take him back. Healing would have to come as a gift.

The process continued over many months and emotional mountains. The twists and turns produced a learning curve amazing even to Graham Kerr. And the drama was to have a completely happy ending.

Part of the healing came as new convictions and callings unfolded to Graham and Treena. "Each day," Graham recalls, "it seemed I became more aware of the world's starving people. Over thirty children a minute die of malnutrition assisted disease—more than seventeen million a year—three times as many as Hitler exterminated during the full span of his 'final solution.' That has something to do with food: the lack of it. On the other hand, there are nations where persons die at the rate of one every forty-three seconds from a different kind of malnutrition: overconsuming the wrong foods."

G raham Kerr began dreaming again. He wondered what could happen if Christian families in America would put the money saved from eating and living more creatively into a program of education and demonstration to enable families in third-world nations to house and feed themselves on carefully managed quarter-acre "farms."

Such dramatic ideas don't succeed without experimentation and models, Graham reasoned. In 1975 the "new" Graham Kerr—still a visionary, adventurous entrepreneur—began testing his new recipe for life. The family liquidated all but the minimum resources a creative life-style would require. They sold their home and most possessions of value, including forgiving debts and assigning over to others book and media contracts worth over three million dollars.

These radical, but not always welcome, changes in the family's life-style were happening fast. In his passion to help the hungry people of the world, Graham would eventually make contact with hundreds of churches, seeking to help other Christian families respond to his call through creative living. Remembering the imbalances which had earlier rocked the family, such as when Graham became dead set against the consumption of any artificial additives, the children struggled with the pressure to go along with each of Dad's new initiatives.

In the early days of their ministry in Colorado, daughter Tessa, now married, and her husband, Joe, were participants. When they decided to pull out, Graham and Treena returned to them $16,530—every cent the young family had put into the joint-ministry venture. It left them with $9.00 in their pockets. Graham wondered, "God, what is this all about?"

Some friends in Palm Springs offered them a room. Graham, Treena, and Kareena, age six at the time, retreated there to rethink their lives and write an autobiography. The legalistic, demanding spirit which characterized much of what Graham had said and done began to fade, and a new and genuine freedom emerged.

G raham's relationship with Andy was renewed as they spent some time fishing and getting to know one another's hearts. Today Andy serves on the board and helps direct the work of a major Christian ministry in Hong Kong. Tears of thanksgiving fill Graham's eyes as he sees his newly married son living and serving with maturity and balance. It's a far cry from the strain during a hillside worship experience when Graham had commanded Andy to stand up with the others and Andy defiantly said no.

Under the umbrella of Youth with a Mission, Graham's visions and drive took on more maturity. His operating methods took on new grace and depth, produced more fruit, and generated fewer casualties. A Creative Lifestyle Network is now one part of the work, helping local churches in the Pacific Northwest train their families in creative living in order to support the mission vision of the church.

The second part is a School of Long-Range Development which is equipping individuals to help the poverty-stricken families they will encounter in developing nations. Partnerships link a church in the U.S. with one in a third-world nation. The entire work is funded by creative life-style changes that enable workers to be trained before they go to serve.

Today the Kerr family is a whole family, and much wiser. Graham has learned that trust with freedom often accomplishes much more with people than pressure. Says Graham, "That's a valuable lesson now that Kareena is in high school." School chums call her "Incredible Kareena" because of her unfailing ability to find the good qualities in almost anyone.

Now that she's dating, Graham has adopted a policy of first interviewing each young man who takes her out. It produces a bit of humor and healthy discomfort, but the expectation that he will care well for a daughter who is very special and loved by her family comes through loud and clear. Kareena feigns minor embarrassment, but Graham knows that deep down she appreciates it.

Graham has wisely given over leadership of the ministry programs to a group of mature and like-minded families. He hasn't made an important leadership decision without their consent for several years. And the project is growing slowly in the mature balance God has taught them to enjoy.

The needs of the world's poor and hungry are more than ever the heartbeat, the cadence to which Graham Kerr is marching. But no man takes as much delight in his grandchildren and real interest in learning now how to be a real son himself to his eighty-year-old mother, Mardi, who lives with them.

Recently Graham was challenged by the thought: If you are

stretched too thin, it could be that you are shallow. Taking the principle to heart, he began carefully deleting some twenty commitments that had gradually plunged him back into life's administrative rapids. "I came to see that mostly *horizontal* obligations filled my days," he says. "I prayed about each one and looked for either God's confirmation to continue or his creative means of leaving gracefully.

"It has taken two years to complete the task, but I am now focused upon a realistic number of commitments I can handle with God's help. And this has greatly enhanced my family time. Being a father is clearly one of the richest gifts God has given me to enjoy."

Servant leadership was a particularly difficult lesson for this "famous" father to put into shoe leather. But Graham Kerr is living proof that in God's grace any father can become a delight to his wife and children, and to God's heart as well.

LUIS PALAU

A father should be a blessing to his children in more than just sharing thoughts and intellectual communication. The father passes on a blessing to his wife and children by the way he walks.

LUIS PALAU
In 1969, a fourth son completed Luis and Pat Palau's family.
Today, two of the boys are away at college.

Luis Palau entered the world on a small farm near Buenos Aires, Argentina. His father, a godly man with missionary zeal, built and sold homes, providing a stable, prosperous, and happy life for the Palau family.

When Luis was ten, without warning, his father became gravely ill. His death several days later changed everything. The family tragedy thrust upon Luis, the eldest son, man-sized responsibilities. There were five sisters left for his mother to raise. She required Luis's help.

Thus, while other Argentine boys were out playing soccer, Luis was being taught family finance, discipline, and spiritual guidance by a most difficult, but effective, tutor—experience.

Today, Luis Palau's substantial reputation as a gospel evangelist blankets the globe. He has preached Christ's good news to awestruck audiences totaling five million and more in thirty-eight nations. Two hundred million have listened to his Festival of the Family crusades over radio and television. This serious youngster from Argentina has come a long way.

In 1961 Luis completed his graduate studies at Multnomah School of the Bible in Portland, Oregon. He had completed college in Buenos Aires and gained experience there in tent evangelism. Talbot Theological Seminary has honored his expertise, leadership, and considerable labors for God's Kingdom with a doctorate degree.

Flights for home still return Luis to Portland where he lives with his wife, Pat, and their teenaged sons, Andrew and Stephen. Two other sons, Kevin and Keith, are studying at Wheaton College in Illinois.

Presently, Luis heads the international outreach ministry bearing his name, the Luis Palau Evangelistic Team.

*I*f I goof up, you're afraid it's going to ruin your reputation. That's why you're worried." It was a terse response to Luis Palau's reprimand of his son. Such an accusation would deeply probe the integrity of any father, but especially one in vocational Christian ministry. Children of religious leaders often feel pressed to shine the brightest and be the best.

This wise father, however, turned that vulnerable moment into an opportunity to teach that only he, and not his sons, must live with the consequences of his choices. "Nothing you do is going to ruin my reputation," Luis replied. "I'm responsible before God for the reputation I build. Your reputation, you build!"

Acting responsibly is just one of the principles underlying the fathering style of this world-famous evangelist. He keeps pressing toward his goal of nurturing steady and strong personal development in each of his four sons—patterns he prays will fall in lockstep with the biblical values he teaches. And because Luis Palau recognizes the dangerous explosions pressuring a child into molds of conformity can trigger, he wisely relies more on well-timed suggestions and the power of personal example than upon fatherly edicts.

This insight is borne perhaps of the hard lessons learned much earlier in his life. Luis was ten when his own father suddenly died, likely of a heart attack. As the oldest son, the burden of helping his mother raise five sisters fell to him.

"I took the role too seriously," he reflects. "If my sisters went out with boys I would tell them to be back at ten o'clock. If they weren't in at ten, I'd be standing at the door. I was probably too hard-nosed about it."

Many of Palau's fondest childhood memories center around his father's deep spiritual commitments. Dad was converted to Christ through the witness of a Plymouth Brethren missionary. Among Luis's treasures are the first Bible and hymnbook given to his father on the occasion of his first "missionary" trip to a nearby village. These mementos were passed to Luis a few years ago by his father's sister when Luis was in Argentina holding a crusade.

Luis nostalgically remembers the numerous times his father stood in church at the Lord's Supper and read from Psalm 95: "O come let us sing for joy to the Lord; Let us shout joyfully to the rock of our salvation." The memory is vividly etched, as are the sounds of his mom pumping out hymns on an inadequate organ in a mission church and his tossing of gospel tracts into outstretched hands from his seat on a bench across the bed of his father's truck while bumping through a new village. These are good memories indeed, recalled of a father whose untimely passing came too soon for a son to notice his less perfect qualities.

While Luis's father was living, his home construction business provided a very comfortable life on the family farm, an hour's drive from Buenos Aires. His dad's death plunged the family from comfort into poverty.

"Suddenly we were renting a house and could hardly pay the rent," reflects Luis. "We owed money to the grocer on the corner. Sometimes it really bothered me. I would shake my fist at the ceiling and ask, 'Why this, why that?' And I admit with great shame that I was sometimes mad at the Lord about the plight of our family.

*B*y nature I am explosive and opinionated," says Luis. "I've changed a lot, I think, but still tend to hold and verbalize strong opinions. And a lot of the change is due to my wife, Pat. Her temperament is the opposite of mine. She is more balanced and even-tempered. She has emotions, but she doesn't respond in kind. The combination of our two personalities continues to complement each one."

Luis Palau conducts evangelistic crusades throughout South America, North America, and Europe. He plans to extend his ministry into Asia. Like many "famous" men who are fathers, he faces unrelenting travel schedules. And to compensate, this dad sets aside exclusive time for his family.

Summers are kept free of long-distance travel—accepting only those summer speaking engagements to which he can bring the whole family. And if he should ever detect that the quality of his family life was being compromised, Luis would not hesitate to set aside his worldwide ministry. That issue has already been decided.

"About four years ago, two of the boys were going through a turbulent period," he recalls. "There was an indication that they might be going off in the wrong direction. Pat and I talked it over, and I made the commitment that if the boys should really become a problem, I would temporarily set aside my international traveling until the situation was resolved and then pick it up again."

As it worked out, Luis did not need to stop traveling. But balancing travel and family considerations will remain his fathering nemesis until his youngest son leaves the nest. That turns the focus now to how time is spent with the family when Dad is at home. It's a soul-searching question which has received the scrutiny of this man, bent first on succeeding as a dad.

"When, because of travel, you have reduced time with your family and then on top of it come home and leave again to play golf with the pastor or swim with somebody, you realize you've got to make a choice," Luis says. "I decided that if I'm going to play tennis, I'll play with the family. If I'm going to swim, I'll swim with the family. Whatever I do when I am at home, I do with my wife and children. Why act like a little boy all your life, having to go out with your buddies to play?

"Really, if you add up the hours I spend with my family and those of any other man who works eight to five at a desk, I probably spend more time with my family than he does. We've made some very conscious decisions about it, but none with a martyr's complex. It's always been a pleasure being with the family, so it has never been like some great burden that I've had to carry."

Luis and Pat try to divide parenting chores in a way that is both fair and effective. Having been raised with three brothers, Pat relates well to her sons and, in Luis's estimation, is by far the more interesting of their two parents.

I think of myself as a bore at home," he allows. "But Pat isn't. She's funny and she's fun and she invents family activities. She does extremely well with the boys. She kids them and jokes more with them than I do. When I saw that, I realized we had no problem. The boys have never seemed to resent that I was on the road, or felt that they missed out that much on life because I was gone." Clearly their attitudes reflect a contribution only Pat could have made to Luis's ministry and fatherly image.

Among the cardinal values Luis wants his children to acquire is respect for others—including their parents. And in a family where Dad's quick temper has been inherited by some of the boys, inevitable conflicts erupt. This father can quickly find himself squared off with a personality cast very much from his own mold.

Just such a confrontation occurred when one of the boys lost his temper and started shouting at Pat. Luis intervened, pulled the boy aside, and said, "Now look. You are not going to treat my wife that way. If any neighbor down the street tried to do that, I'd stop him. She happens to be your mother, but she was my wife before you were born, and she'll continue to be my wife after you are gone. I'm not going to let you treat my wife that way. Do you get it?"

In retrospect, Luis reflects, "My style was not the best, but my son got the point. I wanted to teach him first that I was upset at what he'd done and second that he was to respect her. And if he didn't respect her, he was going to hear from the woman's husband who just happened to be his dad."

A habit of going regularly to God's Word is the premier value Luis yearns for his boys to acquire. He still vividly recalls seeing his own father on his knees, reading the thirty-one chapters of Proverbs. The impression left its mark. Daily, along with his other Bible reading, Luis reads a chapter in Proverbs and finds it invaluable.

"Monday through Friday when I'm home I wake one of the boys about forty minutes earlier than normal," says Luis. "We read the Bible; we share things—no great formality to it. Sometimes they seem half asleep, but those are good times I use to give them a model—to showcase my convictions."

The early morning topics vary. One year was spent on the New Testament. Sometimes dialogue develops out of a helpful Bible study book. The focus is more pump priming than force-feeding. In satisfied tones Luis reflects, "Now I see them doing it on their own, which is really encouraging."

When the boys were younger, the Palaus used Bible storybooks and children's devotionals before bedtime. But Luis doesn't pretend for a moment that the boys always welcomed the ritual. "Some nights you could hardly get through them. Sometimes they made fun of those little questions at the end of the chapters or made dumb remarks. Then other days they were very serious about it. You just have to live with that."

Luis acknowledges that, while being a well-known evangelist, the Palaus don't have family devotions. "We don't knock it. And we say that those who like it should do it. But for us, it just never seemed to work." Perhaps the memories of trying to force devotions upon his sisters to no avail argues well his point.

Luis puts great faith, instead, in the force of example. He and Pat engage in informal Bible study and sometimes personal study with the boys. He likens it to music in their home. Pat often sings at the piano, although the family rarely gathers around to join in. Still, all of the boys but one are interested in music and sing in choral groups. Their love for music came more through osmosis than by direct contact.

Luis also transmits to his boys a concern for the poor—a sensitivity again instilled in him by his own father. The needs of those less well-off were emphasized. "Bragging about our wealth was absolutely out," recalls Palau. His mother believed in trusting God for all the family's needs. She didn't believe in insurance or in saving for retirement. "She felt you should give away everything." And she practiced it. Even today "it's no use giving her things—she just gives them away. She's good. Although she's a very quiet woman, she's had an incredible influence on me."

Luis also encourages in his sons a positive attitude toward the local church. The flaws of a particular minister or church are never emphasized. When negative aspects arise, they are dealt with candidly. "We've tried to teach them a respect and love for the church. To us, spiritual values come first around the Word of God and the church. If there is a problem, we want our boys' first response to be, 'What can I do to help fill the need?' We're not here to criticize the church. We're here to help it."

An atmosphere that encourages questions—the tougher the better— thrives in the Palau home.

An atmosphere that encourages questions—the tougher the better—thrives in the Palau home. "We have never avoided their questions," says Luis. "Sometimes we are sort of shocked, and we laugh about it later—but when the question comes along, we just act like nothing happened. I think the boys will talk about anything with us."

Alongside the spiritual resources, this open atmosphere, as much as anything, has helped the family to cope with the shattering diagnosis in 1981 that Pat had cancer. Currently her prognosis is good. The treatments have apparently been successful, although a few more years must pass before a complete success can be assumed.

"Discovering that my wife had cancer was very difficult," admits Luis. "I think the boys watched us, and they took it like we took it, although they were very quiet about the subject." As painful as the experience has been for every member of the family, it has also been a time for growth. Their grief and concern seemed to draw upon the reserves of love and faith that have been built into this family over the years.

*I*t reinforced everything that we believed and taught and counseled and preached," says Luis. "The question is living it out. Pat is the one who lived it out. To me it's great to feel sorry for yourself and cry and wonder why these things must happen. But the person who actually has the cancer is the one who *really* goes through it."

Ask Luis which father he especially models himself after, and his local pastor and several close friends come to mind. But the example which seems to have shaped him most powerfully is the story of Joseph and Jacob in the Old Testament. "I like the account of Joseph bringing his children to his father and asking Jacob to bless them. That's very moving to me. I think there is something about a father and a grandfather blessing the children. I can't put my finger on it. It relates to the whole idea of being priest in the home—I think there's a spiritual authority there.

"A father should be a blessing to his children in more than just sharing thoughts and intellectual communication," says Luis. "The father passes on a blessing to his wife and children by the way he walks."

For most parents there's a subtle temptation to dream that the kids will follow in their footsteps. It's an obvious compliment to one's own career and success when children choose the same path. Now with two sons in college and two more in high school, career decisions are being made around the Palau household. Surprisingly, Luis and Pat have purposefully downplayed the choices for full-time Christian ministry.

*W*e've actually tried to push them more into secular professions, rather than vocational Christian work," says Luis. "We've urged them to go into medicine or something with the idea of serving the Lord one hundred percent, but as lay people. We just don't believe that full-time Christian work is somehow more godly, spiritual, or superior."

This attitude stems not only from Luis's concern that his achievements might loom too large, but a conviction that the efforts of most full-time workers in the church would be enhanced by a more varied background. "Anyone interested in the ministry should get some secular work experience under his belt," offers Luis. "Not just some summer jobs to pay seminary expenses, but actually going and surviving for a few years in the eight-to-five secular jungle. Then if a person feels called, he or she can go into the ministry."

After persistently encouraging his boys to choose any vocation that truly suits them, each currently seems most inclined to missions and evangelistic work. "They're more outspoken in some areas than we are," he admits. "Even in witnessing. They are far more open about their faith than my wife and I ever were at their ages. I don't think we taught them some of these things. We've simply given our sons opportunity to develop in good Christian fellowships and to meet various missionaries and other Christian workers."

The Palau children pack no delusions of grandeur about the excitement of ministry travel or the joy of meeting the famous people which their father's ministry has attracted. In God's providence the children have already grown beyond Dad and Mom in some areas. And for Luis Palau that simple fact alone has made it all worthwhile.

B.J. THOMAS

It's not important for me to be on the road twenty days every month and let everybody at every club across the country see me. I want my kids to see me.

B.J. THOMAS
Time spent with his family is more important to B.J. than the applause of the crowd.

He was a thin, insecure tenth grader hiding behind an even thinner microphone stand. His raw and untried song styling had not been tested beyond church walls and the high school glee club. But there he was—Billy Joe Thomas (called "B.J." because of the numerous "Billys" on his baseball team) auditioning as a vocalist for The Triumphs, a new band being formed by five guys in his Rosenberg, Texas, neighborhood.

B.J.'s older brother, Jerry, had volunteered him for the tryout. And singing with his own brand of heart, B.J. beat out a fellow with an Elvis Presley imitation to get the job. For the next three years the group, soon called B.J. Thomas and The Triumphs, played to a growing number of restaurant and club audiences in dozens of surrounding Texas towns.

So began the kind of singing career about which most people only fantasize.

In 1966, B.J.'s version of the famous Hank Williams song, "I'm

So Lonesome I Could Cry," sold a million records. Then a concert tour with Gene Pitney's Cavalcade of Stars extended his reputation. "Raindrops Keep Fallin' on My Head" leaped to the top of the charts in 1969—followed by a string of top ten records: "Everybody's Out of Town," "No Love at All," "Mighty Clouds of Joy," "Rock and Roll Lullaby," and "Just Can't Help Believing." Eventually, B.J. won five Grammy awards and sold more than thirty-two million records.

The glitter and the acclaim, however, were only part of the story. B.J. Thomas, the recording star so admired by millions, remained in his own eyes the inadequate little boy who was never able to attract the love of the only fan that really mattered to him—his dad. Accolades couldn't erase the continuing personal sense of failure which haunted this middle child of three. B.J. was caught in the crippling web of emotional patterns modeled by his father, Vernon Thomas. It was a classic replay of poor attitudes about life that were fostered a generation earlier by B.J.'s grandfather.

The root instability and distorted view of manhood evident then were blooming again in B.J.'s low sense of self-esteem. And drug abuse, the all too typical cover-up, was threatening to destroy his family life and career.

It took the birth of his first daughter, Paige, the tenacity of his very spunky wife, Gloria Jean (herself the product of an unstable family), and ultimately the realization that acceptance by God, the Heavenly Father, is the only approval really needed to truly accept oneself, to defuse the time bomb of B.J. Thomas's self-destructive ways.

These dynamics, much more than the prestige of his awards and achievements (including the honor of being the sixtieth musician inducted into the Grand Ole Opry), are now the foundations beneath B.J. Thomas's continuing success story. The arduous process of rebuilding thought patterns and emotional habits has taught B.J. Thomas some pro-

found lessons and set him free to be the kind of husband to Gloria and father to Paige, Nora, and Erin he has always longed to be.

*T*here is a lot of power in a father's words. Singer B.J. Thomas knows all too well: "When you're six years old and your dad says for the hundredth time, 'You dirty, shiftless, worthless bum, get out of here!', you believe it. You say to yourself, 'Man, I'm a dirty bum, and my dad wants me to get out.' That gave me a terribly negative feeling. My idol, my father, didn't like me."

B.J.'s dad, Vernon Thomas—always dictatorial and emotionally remote—had been raised by a father who operated a corn liquor still in the woods around Corsicana, Texas. Vernon was an alcoholic by age thirteen and known as "the biggest hell raiser in the farming communities of East Texas." Having never been nurtured or encouraged himself, it's not hard to understand why he didn't know how to encourage his own children.

As a result, B.J.'s childhood in Houston, Texas, was one frustrating scramble after another to win his father's love and approval. B.J. can remember breaking a glass or falling down to hurt himself— anything that would cause his dad to notice him. "I really wanted Dad to love me," he recalls, "but other than a few yells or a slap on the side of the face, Dad never did seem to respond."

Understandably, B.J. didn't learn much about facing responsibility during childhood, in spite of a hardworking mother who gave it all she could. He wasn't happy and for good reason. One time he got up the courage to ask: "Dad, why are things this way? We don't have things like other families, and we're always fighting." His father's response was, "Billy, I guess you just weren't meant to make it in this life."

Predictably, the effect of the psychological abuse was negative, yet ultimately paradoxical. B.J. was highly motivated to prove that he could be successful. But as one success piled upon another, his low sense of self-esteem kept him from accepting those achievements. Like a badly tangled kite string, this psychological pattern would make soaring to personal highs difficult for most of B.J.'s adult life.

I will always miss those times a child should have with a parent," laments B.J. "My dad never sat still—he always needed to be in motion. He probably could have made a good living for us, working in air conditioning as he did, except that we moved all the time, and he had an alcohol problem. I never had times I could look back on as guiding situations; I've always regretted that. But it has had a positive side. I am motivated to stay around my kids and give them some kind of base."

B.J.'s childhood years were a constant search for ways to win approval. His father liked country and western music, and B.J. quickly sensed this was a way to get Dad's attention. "Ultimately, Dad gave me music," he says. "He was probably my first motivation to be a singer, so I love him for that. It was the only way I could get him to talk with me. I learned songs by Ernest Tubbs and Hank Williams, and I'd sing my tail off to him. And he'd just cry."

Once, when B.J. was in third grade, Dad took the entire family to a Grand Ole Opry performance in Houston to see Hank Williams on stage. B.J. remembers seeing Williams fall to his knees as he played the guitar and sang. "As young as I was, I remember the veins standing out on his neck—and I was sitting all the way in the balcony. I had never seen anybody sing like that—a person who absolutely threw himself into the song. I felt he meant every word he sang."

The example stuck. And singing became the one way B.J. could let himself go. When he sang, and later when he began to perform publicly, he put himself totally into every song. "I felt the music. The words came from my gut. Even today when I sing, I try to do more than entertain. I search for songs I can relate to. When a song speaks to me, then I know it can speak to others as well."

M ost of the time, B.J.'s older brother Jerry was B.J.'s best friend. And when five guys he knew in the neighborhood were forming a band, he volunteered B.J. to audition as their singer. "I went to the garage where they practiced," B.J. recalls. "I had to compete with another singer. He imitated Elvis Presley's style; I just sang like me. They chose me."

The band became known as The Triumphs . . . and later as B.J. Thomas and the Triumphs. Soon B.J. was a solo recording artist with Scepter Records and an increasingly popular concert performer. Flying in the face of his dad's many pessimistic prophecies, B.J. succeeded. But however high his accomplishments, he still had a very low estimation of his own worth. "I could have the number one song in the country and just get depressed about anything," he recalls. "What your folks teach you about yourself, you are!"

A major turning point arrived when his wife, Gloria, gave birth to their first daughter, Paige. Here at last was tangible evidence that B.J. was a worthwhile human being. He had been given another life to care for. "It was the first inkling that I could be a daddy on my own grounds and do things I believed in," he reflects. "I didn't have to follow the pattern."

At this time in his life, a number of contradictory forces were at work. On the one hand, he was a resounding success. His best known hit, "Raindrops Keep Fallin' on My Head," was tearing up the charts. He was in great demand as a concert performer. The new songs he was recording were proving to be successful. And best of all, he was the father of a healthy baby girl. On the other hand, he daily battled with the old demon of low self-esteem, a struggle faced most clearly while away from home on concert tours.

"Musically I was very successful. In a personal sense I was happy, too. But on the road, I could be a loser. I could get high. I could stumble onstage, miss my notes, not make shows—live the classic George Jones life. I was still fighting that feeling of being a born loser.

"Such a route is almost traditional for country and western singers. Hank Williams lived fast and hard, conveying a tragic vulnerability that gave his songs a universal appeal. His death while on the road implied a dedication of legendary proportions to music.

"When music is your life, you're supposed to burn yourself out and die on the back of the bus humming 'I'm So Lonesome I Could Cry,' " B.J. comments. "But nobody hears you hum but yourself. So many people live out a life that's not real because they can't find peace anywhere. That's what I was doing on the road."

Inevitably, strains developed in B.J.'s life. Although earning big bucks, he was in personal trouble. He became a prime target for those career and financial abuses so easily propagated in the entertainment business by incompetent agents with smooth veneers. He and Gloria separated. Only a miracle could end the spiraling cycle of financial problems, drugs, mistakes, and fuzzy

113

thinking. But a miracle—the first of many—happened.

A very sensitive and loving couple stepped into Gloria's life. They listened willingly, lent a car, cleaned up messes, and helped in every way they could. Within a few weeks Gloria experienced the miracle of Christian rebirth. She was changed, and with the help of these same friends, B.J. also discovered a personal walk with Jesus Christ. For the first time, he had the assurance that he was important—ultimately important.

To effectively concentrate on his family, B.J. went into a voluntary semiretirement. The professional sacrifice was substantial.

"It finally dawned on me that God made me like anyone else, that Jesus Christ showed the way for me like anyone else," he recalls. "Suddenly a light bulb came on. I had a different feeling about myself. I didn't hate myself. I wanted to live. Before, I had always wanted to do better, but really deep down I felt like that same kid my dad had taught me I was."

Popular fame and an annual income of fairy-tale proportions had not reassured B.J. that he was a worthwhile human being. But the simple and profound realization that God had created and loved him as a father, did. It enabled B.J. to begin loving himself. He decided to try to reverse his negative life-style and the emotional patterns of the past.

*W*ith a spiritual foundation now in place, strengthened by the warm fellowship of their church family, B.J. and Gloria sought the help of professional counselors in applying Christian principles to the rebuilding of their marriage and family life. Over many months and counseling sessions new insights steadily emerged, followed by understanding and emotional healing.

To effectively concentrate on his family, B.J. went into a voluntary semiretirement. The professional sacrifice was substantial. At the time, his career was at its apex, bringing in about twelve million dollars a year. He had a strong following and the momentum of a string of hits. But he risked it all to step out of the musical limelight and set his personal life straight.

Once B.J. and Gloria knew their lives and marriage were on the right road, they began to plan for another child. After two years of trying to conceive another baby, the opportunity to adopt a Korean orphan was presented to them while assisting in a Nora Lam Sung evangelistic crusade in Taiwan. But was it right? B.J. wondered if they could really provide the kind of stable home this special child would need.

After much soul-searching, the final answer became yes, punctuated by tears of delight when a photograph of Nora, the baby girl, arrived. Less than two weeks after this bundle in tiny, turquoise Chinese pajamas came home, Gloria discovered she was pregnant. She gave birth to another daughter, Erin.

With three kids, B.J.'s commitment to stay home became firmer than ever. In retrospect he reflects, "I feel good about it—being able to say I made a sacrifice for my family. I made a choice to stay home. It's not important for me to be on the road twenty days every month and let everybody at every club across the country see me. I want my kids to see me."

B.J. has since returned to his career. He's determined this time to keep a tight rein on his travel schedule and when home to spend very special times with each of the girls. The balance hasn't been perfect, but it's constantly improving. "A lot of times it's hard to remember who you are when you get caught up in everything people are doing," he says. "I've found myself on airplanes and out of town when I could have been home. That happens. You learn from it, though."

A nger, and its proper expression, is still a concern and an ongoing area of reconstruction in B.J.'s life and marriage. As an entertainer, there have been a few blowups onstage. In everyday life, he sometimes loses the battle in the form of inordinate rage at an inconsiderate driver or even an undercooked hamburger.

"It kills you to hand out that kind of abuse," he says. "It'll cost me something—I may lose a couple of pounds over it."

Concern about controlling his harsher emotions sometimes spills over into an unwanted control of his positive emotions. Having had a father who found it hard to show affection, B.J. emphasizes the expression of love. "If you hold in the positive feeling of love for someone long enough and don't share it, it atrophies."

B.J. feels a little argument can be just as important as a kiss. "If you don't let somebody know he or she really bugged you, then you have to harbor it and will have a big explosion or something later. And maybe it's just as important to give somebody a hug even if you don't mean it. It's a mystery—maintaining personal relationships and still being honest. It's hard to do. You have to stay with it all the time."

These days B.J. has little use for anger in parenting. He does at times lose his temper and get mad at the kids, but feels that his anger does little to motivate them towards better behavior.

*I*n his childhood home, children were to be seen and not heard. Behavior was strictly regimented. So with their own children, B.J. and Gloria try to create an atmosphere in which the girls are first encouraged to accept themselves as they are and second to behave in acceptable manners. The priority of helping each child understand good behavior is then in her own best interest.

In meting out discipline, B.J. is especially sensitive to seeing things from the child's point of view. It's the best way he knows to avoid repeating the parenting mistakes he lived with as a child. "If I didn't understand my third daughter, I guess I possibly would treat her the way I was treated," he says. "I would stifle her."

Like all fathers, B.J. grapples with how much to demand from his children and how much to let them learn from their own mistakes. Tending to be impatient and a strong competitor, he tries to control his urge to force behavior. B.J. recalls the first time Paige was doing poorly at school. Her grades dropped suddenly, and she wasn't interested in doing her homework. He and Gloria forced Paige to do her work, only to realize that while the task got done, she was dragging her feet all the way.

"Finally we came to the realization that it's got to be her choice," he reflects. "If she wanted to be in the third grade when she was twenty, we guessed she could do that. So we said, 'Hey, your homework from now on is your own responsibility. If you don't want to do it, don't do it.' Of course, the next report card was the classic straight A thing."

*D*uring her transition from grammar school to junior high, Paige's grades dropped off again. Again Dad and Mom stressed the natural consequences; if she neglected her homework her grades would fall. With low grades, chances were she wouldn't get the basics upon which she could build the rest of her education. "We just let her know that we think she's a better student than that. It's her responsibility, but we expect better from her." Again patience paid off and the prescription worked.

B.J. still struggles with the balance between controlling his children and accepting them where they are. He feels he's probably too lenient. "The way I was raised and the way I raise my kids are completely opposite sides of the road. A lot of times, I go overboard where another person might be more of a disciplinarian. That's maybe where Gloria comes in—she's more of a disciplinarian than I am."

B.J.'s concert schedule and Gloria's responsibilites as his business manager require that the Thomases employ a full-time nanny. But B.J. compensates by being as active a father as possible. Typically, when he's home he cooks breakfast for the kids and, at the end of the day, gets them off to bed.

"I didn't change a diaper with Paige," he says. "It wasn't the 'manly' thing to do. Only later did I gain such a good feeling about myself I could do anything."

The impact of affluence on the family also concerns B.J. Managing considerable sums of money is a problem many people would welcome, seeing money as a solution to problems, not a cause. But B.J. knows differently and is concerned that his daughters will understand that money is relatively unimportant.

I want my kids to realize that money is not happiness. A lot of people who don't have as much money as we have are way happier than we are. I've got kids who don't want anything for Christmas," he continues. "Paige even asked us to back off on the presents a bit. I think my two little ones will get a good perspective on it."

In addition to wealth, the visibility of being a show-biz family places a special pressure on the children as they grow older. "Most people don't realize that entertainers are just regular people," B.J. muses. "It's a glamorous business, but the spotlight time is very small. Because people are in awe of what I do for a living, it does put undue pressure on my children." B.J. expects eventually to move the family to an old farmhouse he has acquired near Nashville, reasoning that entertainers are not so unusual there.

B.J. considers it his loss that he has few close friends outside the music business. He has found it hard to trust close relationships. "I

117

know that it has been my own choosing," he says. "I think I'm really more lonely today than I have to be, because I never learned well how to carry out intimate relationships. I hope my kids won't have that problem.

"We've tried to teach Paige that God made everybody. She needs to have love for everyone and not just her friends. So many times kids her age will have a true hatred for a kid who just looks different—a fat girl, or a kid with an impediment." He wants her to love others—not an attitude that was a part of his upbringing.

B.J. Thomas's own painful childhood has unquestionably motivated him to do much better for his three daughters. He remains tenacious in his quest to break the effects of the vicious cycle of low self-esteem. Quite easily it could have been passed on to yet another generation.

"A lot of times I just stand in awe of my kids and have to slap myself to be sure I'm not dreaming," he says. "They don't feel like I felt as a kid. They're free, and I think that's great."

JOSH MC DOWELL

When they've seen me do something wrong I must quickly go to them to apologize and seek forgiveness. It's what they must see me model if they are going to mature into sensitive persons, able to admit and set right their mistakes.

JOSH MC DOWELL
The peaceful setting of their California mountain home
enhances many special McDowell family moments.

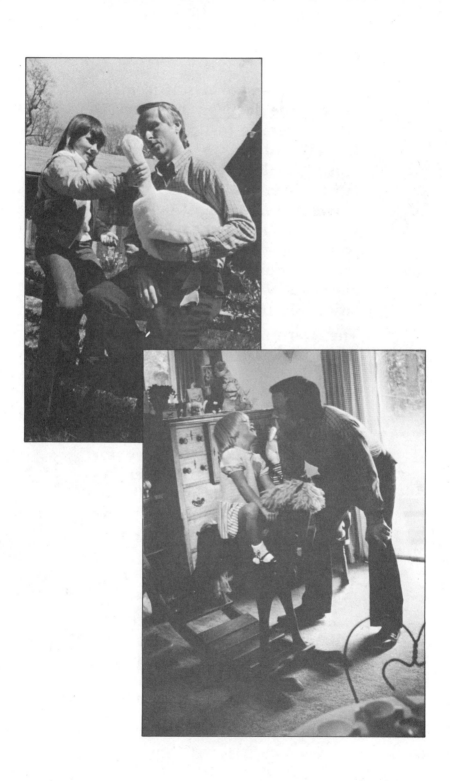

"I used to assert myself to make up for the lack of attention at home," recalls Joslin David Mc-Dowell—known to everyone as "Josh." "I hardly ever knew my father sober until I was nineteen or twenty years of age. As a result, I never had much of a relationship with him—you know: going fishing . . . doing things together. I never knew what a father-son relationship ought to be."

The warm, lighthearted chatter which now fills the McDowells' rustic family room confirms that history is not repeating itself here. This respected author, university lecturer, film personality, and traveling representative for Campus Crusade for Christ enjoys a quality relationship with his wife Dottie and their three young children, Kelly, Sean, and Katie.

Josh was youngest in his family and grew up on their dairy farm in Michigan with a slightly older brother, Jim. Another brother, Wilmont, was twenty years older than Josh. And his sister Shirley, twenty-three years older, seemed more like a mother than a sister to him.

In school, Josh earned high grades and excelled in sports. It compensated for his stuttering when under pressure—the legacy of a well-meaning second-grade teacher who tried to force him to be right-handed.

Josh's mother died during his stint in the Air Force. Later, while still in the service, he sustained a serious head injury. After a full recovery, his aptitude for mechanics provided success at several jobs. Josh eventually enrolled in college and set his sights on a law career. His game plan was to be elected the governor of Michigan in twenty-five years.

But God had other purposes for this highly motivated young man, and used the gutsy retort of a Christian coed at Kellogg College to send him digging into the reliability of the Bible and historicity of Jesus Christ's resurrection. The evidence he uncovered drove Josh to conclude that Jesus of Nazareth was indeed the Lord and Savior of the universe. Josh surrendered to him control of his life.

Another severe accident in college could have taken Josh's life. Instead, it opened the door to his father's spiritual conversion and ultimately to Josh's choice of a theological seminary over law school.

Today, well over seven million university students and faculty at more than six hundred campuses in sixty-two countries have heard Josh speak. In the words of Billy Graham, "Josh has a unique ability to deal clearly and directly with many of the intellectual issues facing college students today."

Josh's impeccable logic and sensitive insights have helped people worldwide through more than twenty best-selling books, nineteen films, and two television specials. At home, however, this dad is perhaps best known for his playful antics in the Jacuzzi and his bedtime snuggles.

S tick around and you'll discover a unique bedtime ritual at the McDowell home. When Daddy is home, even if there's company, he excuses himself about seven o'clock to go to bed. Josh and his three children spend the first half hour in the Jacuzzi just off the master bedroom. The warm, pulsating water seems to loosen not only tense muscles but conversation, as Dad poses questions and they talk easily about the events of the day.

"Family Feud" on the bedroom TV is frequently the next focus as they play along, trying to best the on-screen contestants. Then everyone piles onto the queen-size bed to talk, play around, snuggle, and fall asleep. "The kids are not only getting older, but heavier," muses Josh, after toting them off to their own beds. "But it's more than worth it. It's the one sure time I have each day to talk with my children."

Talking, listening, and approaching aggressively his fathering responsibilities are part of Josh McDowell's most important life commitments—an assignment made several times more difficult by a travel schedule which, in spite of recent trimming, still finds him on the road fifty percent of his time.

According to Josh, he was "desperate" when Kelly, his first child, was born. "I never had a loving and creative example in my own father. I can't remember even once his hugging my mother or my ever desiring to be with him. But suddenly, here I was a father, and I didn't know what to do. So I started watching others, gathering information—reading every book and newsletter like *Dads Only* I could get my hands on, and sitting down trying to think creatively."

As a result, in spite of his extensive travels away from home, Josh enjoys a relationship with his children many dads with eight-to-five jobs might envy. It's been built upon the same energy, meticulous study, logic, and planning which have made Josh one of America's favorite authors and most respected authorities in Christian apologetics.

Most mornings when he's home, Josh takes Kelly, Sean, and Katie out for breakfast on their way to school. "It costs a little money," he says, "but it gives me about forty-five minutes to an hour of uninterrupted time with them." To pinch pennies they all order the same thing so it can be divided up—pancakes one time, an egg dish or French toast the next.

During the ten-minute drive to the cafe, Josh quizzes the kids on theological issues. "This morning I asked about the Holy Spirit. 'Who is the Holy Spirit? What part of the Trinity is he? Why did the Holy Spirit come? What does the Holy Spirit do? and when does the Holy Spirit come into your life?' Even Katie, my youngest, gets questioned. She doesn't usually have the right answers, but she's learning.

"Between the time we order and our food arrives, I usually do one of two things. I may choose to read a Bible passage and ask questions, emphasizing a basic truth from it. For example, this morning we read the familiar story of David and Goliath, and discussed how, as with David and his small stone, God can take our individual strengths and multiply them.

The other thing I may do which excites me is what I call 'value determination'—helping the kids decide what their values are. We make a game of it: I describe a moral or ethical situation and then ask them how they would respond. After correcting or reinforcing their response, I point out an aspect of God's character which supports the correct behavior in that situation. Thus, instead of a Bible passage being the sole support for the rightness of an action, I focus on God's character. That makes the motivational source a Person instead of a book, albeit an essential one.

"Next, I'll describe a situation: say, for example, when somebody lied. Then I'll ask, 'Why is it wrong to lie?' One of the kids will answer, 'Because the Bible says, "Thou shalt not lie." ' 'But why does the Bible say, "Thou shalt not lie?" ' I ask. Of course, the answer is, 'Because God is truth.'

"Then I'll continue, 'Let's imagine there's a Coke machine over there, and you put in thirty-five cents and you get back not only the Coke but the thirty-five cents, too. What do you do with the money?'

"The first time I asked, Sean said, 'I'd give it to the cashier.' So I pressed and asked, 'Why? It was your money.' 'That's right,' he hesitated. Then I taught him that once you exchange your money for something else it's no longer your money. I asked, 'What would it be if you kept it? . . . Stealing! Is stealing wrong? Yes, the Bible says, "Thou shalt not steal." ' From there we went on to the nature of God again."

Josh has taken a similar approach to teaching the concept of God's grace in relationships with people. He asks, "What's the first thing you would do if you saw a classmate cheating?" The kids responded, "Tell the teacher." To which Josh retorted, "Absolutely not," and offered this explanation:

"God deals with us in grace and is most patient in how he teaches us. The first thing to do is to tell the person that cheating is wrong.

126

If you don't, and the person later steals other information and valuables, it becomes partially your fault. God says in the book of Ezekiel that if you see a brother in sin and you correct him, then whether he corrects himself or not, it's his problem. But if you see a brother in sin and do not correct him, then his blood is on your hands.

"So," Josh instructs, "first tell the person it's wrong and he shouldn't do it. Then, if you see it happen again and again, you should tell him that because you love him and you're a friend, you must report it to the teacher or principal. That way you're dealing in grace . . . just the way God deals with us. God doesn't immediately take us to the woodshed and thrash us, spiritually speaking."

Josh takes his children along whenever possible as he runs simple errands, because it offers a chance for them to see how he treats people, reacts, and handles himself when he blows it or someone offends him. "For a while," Josh recalls, "I thought I would appear weak to my children if they saw me lose my cool and make mistakes. Now I realize that when they've seen me do something wrong or I've been wrong in how I've handled something with them, I must quickly go to them to apologize and seek forgiveness. It's only right, and it's what they must see me model if they are going to mature into sensitive persons, able to admit and set right their own mistakes."

*D*emonstrating to his children that they are a top priority when his work requires so much public speaking and time with other people presents a challenge to Josh. On more than one occasion when the children were younger, they helped him out by taking things into their own hands.

Josh was speaking to Trinity College's largest chapel crowd ever, when Sean ran up from his seat and said, "Daddy, I want to be with you." To the audience Josh explained, "Excuse me, but my children have priority over even you, so if you don't mind, my son wants to be with me." He sat Sean on the podium. Almost immediately the audience became more responsive.

On another occasion Josh was speaking to a rather hostile crowd on the Free Speech Platform at Brown University. Suddenly Kelly broke away from the person caring for her, jumped up on the riser, hugged and kissed Josh's leg, and just looked up at him. Again the crowd's mood changed dramatically. Cameras clicked and the photo hit all the area newspapers.

When on the road, Josh calls home every day, sometimes twice, to talk with Dottie and each of the children. "Because of the expense, I used to rush it and cut them off," Josh says. "Then I began to realize that my children wanted to share things with me. So now I probe with questions like, 'How's the day going? What did you learn today?' and let them talk.

"We probably communicate more than a lot of married couples that are together daily," Dottie suggests. "But that doesn't make it any less difficult for me," says Josh, "when I discover that one of the kids has had a hard day or is sick or hurt—or on the other hand has achieved an honor or passed a personal milestone. It's hard not to be there, because I'm usually unable to help at that moment in any meaningful way."

Sometimes, especially in recent years, Josh has canceled meetings just to be home for an important event. "Sean is the hero on his soccer team," Josh beams. "If they score nine goals, he'll have made seven of them. I was able to arrange for two different professional soccer coaches I know to spend time with him. It's really paid off. The first game I went to, every time he'd kick the ball, he'd look over at me," Josh remembers. "It was just thrilling . . . even the shots he missed."

Learning how to prepare himself to reenter the flow of family life when returning home from a week or two on the road has made a big difference for everyone. "Two days ago, when I flew in from the east coast, about an hour out of San Diego I started telling myself, 'Now when you hit the airport, you start thinking of the family. Put business out of your mind and focus on what you're going to do with the children when you get to the house. The first day home I try to make everything revolve around the family.

"If I return on a school day, I'll fly all night if I have to—praying all the while the plane won't be late—just so I can be there to pick the kids up from school and spend the next hour with them. We'll go to the park and talk. Or maybe we'll order chocolate milk shakes at the old marble-topped soda fountain in the drugstore.

Surprisingly, for most of his life, interpersonal relationships have been one of Josh's weakest areas. He wishes he had learned a lot earlier to communicate with the children— especially Kelly. Josh recalls that for the first three or four years he didn't really listen to her. "It got to the point where if she wanted to talk to me, she'd go 'ding-dong, Daddy, ding-dong.' But even when she was doing that I didn't realize how serious it was. I'd stop and say, 'Yeah,' and then I'd go on.

"Dottie really helped me with this. She kept hammering home, 'Honey, you're not communicating.' I'd say, 'Yes, I am.' 'No, you don't listen,' she would counter. 'Your mind is off somewhere else. One of the children or I will start to share something with you, and you'll cut us off. We'll ask you something and you won't even give us an answer.'

"Gradually I realized that Dottie was right. I would usually hear what was being said, but my mind would be going a mile a minute. I'd look like I was listening, but I found out that Dottie and the kids could see right through me. I had to learn that respect begins with listening," Josh laments.

"Some people will feel it's awful, but I had to write myself notes: 'Listen to your children. Pay attention to them.' To correct the habit, every week for about two years, no matter where I was, I forced myself to find somebody and just listen to them for thirty minutes. I'm thankful that I've changed a great deal in this area."

Josh also wishes he would have learned a lot earlier that failure to schedule time purposefully with his children usually means they don't get any. "It was my loss as well as theirs," he laments. "It's only been in the past two or three years that I've really made this work for me.

"One day Dottie brought home the point when she said, 'Honey, if we show an interest in our children now, they will show an interest in us later. If we take time with our children now, they will take time with us later.' That hit me right between the eyes."

For many years Josh carried deep within him the fear that he could never really love someone, that he would always be on the go and wouldn't ever really choose to take the time to nourish a deep relationship. However, as he dated Dottie and his love for her began growing, the fear began to subside. He had never seen the love he wanted in his folks or anyone else except for some couples he came to know well during seminary days.

Even after marrying Dottie, Josh had to work at liberating his expressions of love, and feels he was especially fortunate that Dottie would only let things go so long before speaking up about them. "If she hadn't voiced her feelings, our marriage would have been shot years ago," Josh says.

It's just that sort of appreciation and pride in Dottie that Josh makes sure the kids see and take part in. Before a recent wedding anniversary he talked with the kids about Dottie's two favorite foods—swordfish and real Italian spaghetti. They knew about the secret arrangements he made to have the chef at the Boardwalk (their favorite restaurant in Laguna Beach, California) prepare a swordfish dinner on their anniversary eve. And they also knew Dad had reserved a table at Salerno's for a special spaghetti dinner the following night.

For many years Josh *carried deep within him the fear that he could never really love someone.*

"Do you know why I'm doing things like these for your mother?" Josh quizzed the kids. The answer he wanted came back, "Yeah, because you love her."

When leaving on a trip, Josh frequently hides "love coupons" around the house. Once found by Mom, they are collected on the refrigerator door. Sometimes the kids will remind Josh, "Daddy, you've got to do that now; you gave a love coupon to Mom."

Josh believes Dr. James Coleman, a professor of sociology at the University of Chicago, is right when he says, "I think we are becoming the first species in the history of the world which is unable to care for its young. Overall, child rearing is one of the biggest casualties of the modern age that is being ushered in by this generation." Perhaps this is why Josh McDowell is so attentive to both the big concerns and the details of nourishing his family—in spite of the constant pressures of speaking and manuscript deadlines.

Positive self-esteem runs deep in the McDowell children. Sean likes to bicycle alongside while Dad is jogging, and appreciates his dad's help with strong pushes up long hills. When Josh asked why he thought Dad helped him like that, Sean's reply was, "Because I'm special."

Josh McDowell's approach to fathering is guided by a simple focus. "I want to be the type of person that my children can respect. That takes a whole lot," he says, "especially a responsive attitude towards God. Everything revolves around that."

ROGER STAUBACH

I haven't completely figured out being a parent by any means. The one thing I do know is that the bottom line is love—they have to know you love them.

131

ROGER STAUBACH
Though the Staubach clan admits some drawbacks of having a famous dad, they also recognize the privileges—like meeting Vice President George Bush.

"He was super," said Dallas Cowboys coach Tom Landry, following the final game of the final season of Roger Staubach's NFL career. "What can you say about a guy who's done it so many times?" In eleven seasons, Staubach brought the Cowboys from behind in the fourth quarter to win twenty-one games—fourteen of them in the last two minutes or overtime.

Tight end Billy Joe DuPree observed: "The one thing that will always stand out in my mind about Roger is that he never knew when it was over. At the end of a game, even if we were down by twenty points, he'd be standing there by himself trying to figure out a way we could win it." Even playing sandlot ball as a kid, Roger Staubach sought the action—to be whenever possible the playmaker or key contributor.

In a sport often criticized for dishing out extraordinary physical punishment, it seems incredible that one of its heroes would attract monikers like "Lieutenant Fair and Square," "Mr. Straight

Arrow," and "Galahad of the Gridiron." The nicknames describe Roger Staubach's integrity, yet he detests the corresponding dull, one-dimensional, white-knight, out-of-touch image they also bring to mind.

That Staubach's life has been anything but fairy tale is confirmed by a glance at his right hand—his passing hand. The fingers look almost arthritic—knuckles like knots. And the scars on the back of the hand and wrist bear silent witness to football's relentless pounding. Bart Starr once observed that from the first heavy blow of the preseason games to a month after the Super Bowl, a first-string quarterback never stops aching.

Roger is also very much in the thick of the fray as a parent. Although he was an only child, he and wife Marianne have five children. Three are now teenagers, and Roger knows that parenting perfection is at least as difficult as completing fifty-yard touchdown passes. He also believes that family success is made from the same ingredients as a winning season—well-conceived game plans, teamwork, concentration, adjustments, lots of hard work, and God's blessing.

As a United States Naval Academy midshipman, Roger won the Heisman Trophy in 1963. Following his tour of service, including a year in Vietnam, he became a Dallas Cowboys superstar for eleven seasons, completing 1,685 passes out of 2,958 attempts for fifty-seven percent completed. He led the National Football League in passing in 1973, 1978, and 1979, and still stands as the NFL's highest ranked quarterback.

Today, the help of a personal assistant is still required to answer his fan mail. Roger is president of his own commercial real estate firm and is involved with groups like the Fellowship of Christian Athletes, the Salvation Army, the American Diabetes Association, the Paul Anderson Youth Home.

On gym equipment in his garage, Roger Staubach works out to keep his six-foot-three frame in the athletic condition he enjoys. And in a

way, he is still quarterbacking—as dad for a first-rate team called the Staubach family. They play in a north Dallas stadium called home. As you might expect, they're winners!

Something in the nature of things makes a good man seem less interesting than a bad one. Sports commentator Phyllis George once said as much in contrasting the life-style of Roger Staubach with that of Joe Namath.

The comparison made Roger bristle: "I enjoy sex as much as Namath—only with one woman." His life-style is usually perceived, he says, "as if the things I believe in reduce the enjoyment of life when compared to the wine-women-and-song philosophy. To me that's incredible. Having peace of mind and having relationships that are meaningful are the substance of life."

It's no accident that family relationships are among the most meaningful to Roger Staubach. This flows quite naturally from the home in the Cincinnati suburb of Silverton, Ohio, where he grew up. "I played basketball across the street at Tom Brannen's house and football in the Beins' backyard along with their nine kids. Family life was filled with richness, wonder, and challenge for me then, as it is now." If any of this crimps his style, Roger is certain he's the better man for it.

Staubach's father, a manufacturer's rep for a shoe leather and thread company, was his greatest hero. "He was easygoing," Roger remembers, "the kind of guy you wanted as a friend because nothing seemed to bother him." That laid-back, noncompetitive bent may be one of the reasons Dad infrequently attended the games in Roger's young athletic career. The other reason was balance. His parents stressed keeping sports in balance with the rest of life.

Roger always delighted in playing the hot sports," his father once observed. "He liked situations where the outcome of the game depended on him—the pressure positions that others might avoid."

"That's the way I was as a kid," Roger affirms. "I wanted the ball hit to me, I wanted to take the shot, to run with the ball. I liked being good because there was a certain status that came with it. But there was always something inside that made me press to be better. Maybe I got the competitive drive from my mom. Whatever she did, singing or playing the piano, she wanted to be the best."

Roger's parents, by strength of example more than by stern discipline, established guidelines and set the tone for their only child. This, coupled with their devout participation as Christians in the Roman Catholic Church and Roger's education in parochial schools, gave him a life-forming framework. "The love I felt from my parents, the Bible reading we would do together at night, the examples they set for me, and my Christian faith, all were instrumental in molding me into the kind of person I am today," he says.

Roger recalls with special clarity his parents' convictions concerning racial prejudice. "A black family moved close to our neighborhood, and many folks became quite upset about it. One night I listened from another room to the heated discussion among neighbors in our living room. My mother gave one of the most unbelievable speeches. She just completely chastised them for being worried about it. And she didn't have anything in her past to cause her to do it—just her obedience to Scripture and her Christian faith." Such an example—perhaps the sense that this was the Staubach way of doing things—shaped Roger's behavior far more than the fear of punishment.

Once, several of Roger's friends urged him to go with them to a carnival. To get there he would have to cross Ohio Street, a busy thoroughfare he had been specifically forbidden to cross. The temptation was strong. He knew his parents wouldn't have minded his going to the carnival, but he didn't. "I wouldn't cross that street because of my parents—not that I feared them or feared I'd be punished, but because I loved them and didn't want to disappoint them."

As a child, Roger was for a time attracted to stealing. In first grade he recalls taking, of all things, a crucifix and a saint's medallion from a religious supply store. About the same time he also stole sixty cents from a neighbor's table. The booty was hidden in a dresser drawer, where every morning he'd look at it. "Its very presence was an indictment," he remembers. "I grew more miserable every day."

Finally, while lying on the living room couch one evening, Roger burst into tears. "My mother thought I was sick until I told her what I'd done. I realized that my parents had taught me better than that," he says. "I was a thief. My remorse was overwhelming. Mother told the neighbor, Mrs. Cross, what I'd done and made me apologize to her. It was the most embarrassing time of my life, and I dreaded ever seeing the Crosses again."

In teaching his children about Christianity, Roger has been careful to separate the essentials from the peripheral matters. He knows they have to think out their faith on their own terms. Individual differences are not only acknowledged, they're encouraged. But his approach is not so open-ended that he wouldn't be concerned if they left the faith. "If all of a sudden they said they didn't want to practice their Catholic faith, I'd be very disappointed. But the big thing is, I would be distraught if they didn't believe in Jesus Christ."

Roger and Marianne want each of the children to get all they can out of life's stages, especially childhood. So they sensitively seek to counter those pressures which push kids too fast into adulthood. "We emphasize that once a certain level is attained, it's only natural to want more," says Roger. "That's just life. Some new experiences are healthy and some aren't. Kids don't realize that. There's so much of life ahead; if they gobble up too much at once, they grow too quickly." The Staubachs try to help their children grow at a pace that is matched to their maturity and level of responsibility.

"There's so much of life ahead; if kids gobble up too much at once, they grow too quickly."

At this point, Roger could well afford to give the kids most anything they might want. But he and Marianne are very concerned that the children develop a sense of gratitude for what they have. "A lot of people don't spoil their children because they can't," says Roger. "We have to make a conscious effort not to overdo it. Sometimes they're not as appreciative as they probably should be. It's just not our human nature to be grateful.

We want more. I guess we're all that way."

Besides wealth, Roger's fame has also presented difficulties for the Staubachs. When Roger was still a quarterback, there was the consistent danger that Sunday's Cowboys performance would haunt the kids at school the next day. "Fortunately, our four daughters weren't expected to be into football as much as sons would have been," comments Roger.

For son Jeff, Roger is concerned that his own past accomplishments not put a lot of pressure on his only boy. "I've seen sons handicapped by having famous fathers. I don't want it to happen to Jeff. I want him to become Jeff Staubach with no mention of who his father is." That will probably include discouraging Jeff from playing football, unless he should happen to exhibit an exceptional talent and the self-esteem to weather the inevitable comparisons. "I want Jeff to enjoy the excitement and challenge of athletics without the pressure of competing against my image. I've found a great deal of joy and excitement in sports. I hope all my children can have the same experience."

*T*he communication style between Roger and Marianne is low-key. He could probably count on one hand the times he's raised his voice at her. "We're both even-tempered, and I'm not an aggressive person at home," says Roger. "If I get real mad, I tend to sulk more than to get violent. Marianne and I keep things inside us—not in an unhealthy way—but we have a tendency when we're upset not to scream or argue with each other. That's just our nature."

Because it happens so seldom, the few times they have raised their voices have created a deep impact. Roger feels communication cannot be emphasized enough: "Ours is not nearly what it should be at times, and we're constantly at work on it. We have a very good relationship. It's just that we're never satisfied with it completely, and I think that's healthy. It keeps us growing."

"We're not overly strict parents," Roger assesses. "There is organization in our family structure, responsibilities for everyone within the unit. Over the years Marianne has kept a chart in the kitchen to remind the kids of their duties—setting the table and clearing it, doing dishes, and taking care of their bedrooms—the everyday things you find in so many homes.

"Neither of us is a fanatic about demanding perfection in our children's behavior, or inflexible over an occasional exception to the rules. It's normal for every kid to test his parents at some point just to see how far he can go—what he can get away with. Yet I believe a child feels better and more secure in knowing there are boundaries beyond which he or she is not allowed to go."

With a house full of teenage daughters each stretching for her own individual independence, identity, and life-style, Roger is finding himself in new and somewhat uncharted fathering waters. "It's a hard period for Roger," says Marianne, "because, not having any sisters, he has no idea of how girls react. Half the time he doesn't know how I'm going to react, much less a teenage girl."

Facing those moments when one of the children has deliberately violated a cardinal Staubach family value tests Roger's confidence and security as a father. "Of course, they always feel extremely bad," he reflects, "and I'm sure Marianne and I feel even worse.

"Once I get past my anger and sense of disappointment, I find myself feeling that somehow, somewhere, I must have failed as a parent. It's hard to remember that children are not possessions, but unique individuals created by God with their own capacity to choose for themselves. Knowing this and getting comfortable with it when older children choose against your wishes, I'm finding, is a sobering reality.

"What hurts most is when a mistake they make can't be reversed. That's when my love, not based on performance, must really shine. God deals with me that way—caring more about who I am than what I've done—forgiving me. I'm now more convinced than ever that this kind of acceptance and love must be the bedrock of our family and of my parenting. Events have tested my understanding of this truth and, thankfully, I'm learning."

Hard things and difficult emotions aren't strangers to Roger or to the Staubach family. In 1971 tragedy struck when a baby girl was stillborn. "The delivery was normal," recalls Roger. "The eight-pound, three-ounce daughter was perfect in every respect, except that she was dead." Doctors theorized that the umbilical cord was short and she strangled. Her grave marker reads "Baby Girl Staubach." Reflects Roger, "She was gone before we knew her."

Neither of Roger's parents was able to follow his football career to its conclusion. His dad died just before Roger's second season in

Dallas, and the death of his mother was another difficult time for the family. Grandma had lived with the Staubachs for the final months after it was discovered she had terminal cancer.

Through much pain, the same faith she had taught Roger sustained her. "The thought that her remaining time was short overwhelmed me one day when I was visiting her in the hospital. I burst out crying in front of her. She motioned me toward her and whispered, 'Please don't do that. I'll be fine. Look at it this way— you'll always have a friend in heaven.' I learned a lot about love from her."

Retirement from football hasn't reduced the demands upon Roger's time. He finds he still must work at keeping his travel schedule from damaging the quality of his family life. Marianne often travels with him, and when circumstances allow, he likes to take one of the kids along as well. Individual time with a son or daughter is scarce when your attention must be spread among five children.

"Basically I'm a homebody," Roger admits. "I don't like to travel. I like to be around home and make sure everything's okay. I wouldn't enjoy being away from the family and working all the time. That wouldn't be fun."

To give himself as much family time as possible, Roger has located his office just two minutes from home. Often he comes home for lunch. Still, he feels his greatest failing is not giving the children all the attention they want and need. Old patterns sometimes still haunt him. "I'd be watching game films," he recalls, "and my daughter would come in to tell me about something that happened in school. I'd say, 'Not now; can't you see I'm busy?' She'd go away. Then an hour later I'd think, 'What have I done?' I'd go and find her up in her bedroom and try to tell her how sorry I was."

Like many fathers, Roger has faced the frustration of setting aside time to be with one of the kids, only to discover that the child wasn't feeling communicative. His simple solution has been effective. "I go and sit in their rooms with them," he says. "I just sit there and all of a sudden they open up and start talking. That's the most fun."

*T*hroughout his life, the competitive spirit of Roger Staubach has kept him in the thick of things. The challenge of fathering, he acknowledges, has required at times far more discipline and self-control than his football or business careers have ever demanded. And Roger Staubach still allows no pretense. "I haven't completely figured out being a parent by any means," he says. "I'm learning all the time. The one thing I do know is that the bottom line is love—they have to know you love them."

KEN TAYLOR

Not every child turns out the way we hope and dream.

It is dangerous for parents to say "I want my child to do this or be that."

KEN TAYLOR
Ken's life has changed considerably since the days when
shipping Bibles from the garage was a family project!

Some children become well known because of their father's achievements. And some fathers bask in recognition due to the success of their offspring. But the case of Kenneth N. Taylor and his ten children is unique—it is what he did for them that brought him fame wherever Bibles are bought and read.

Ken Taylor is the man who made The Living Bible possible. His easy to understand, thought-for-thought paraphrasing of the Scriptures is recognized as the work which ushered in a whole new generation of translations. When the Evangelical Christian Publishers Association gave Dr. Taylor its Gold Medallion, a recognition of highest achievement, the assembled members of the publishing industry gave Ken not one, but two, standing ovations.

The Bible continues to be the world's best-seller—and The Living Bible points the way. More than twenty-nine million copies have been sold in twelve years, and even today, with many translations available in a variety of forms and packages, The Living Bible still sells more than a million copies a year.

It was Ken Taylor's concern for his family that started this momentous work. Every evening after supper, he conducted family devotions. He would read the Bible, ask questions, and have each child pray.

"Why did we have family devotions?" he asks. "I was brought up with them, and I never had any serious teenage problems. Neither did my brothers. So I assumed that was the magic touch.

"I would read the King James Version and ask my questions. Often the kids would just sit there, as though they didn't understand the words. I thought there must be an easier way—and the Lord just put it into my mind: 'Why not translate the thoughts instead of words?'

"By taking each thought and putting it in simple, understandable English, I could produce in the minds of my children the same thoughts that the writers of the original Scriptures produced in the Hebrew or Greek."

Ken began experimenting. He read a verse and asked himself, "What is the thought of this verse? How can I express it so the children will understand it?" He put seven or eight verses into simple English and took them to the family. He recalls, "When I asked my questions, instead of just shrugging their shoulders, the children could answer! They knew what I had read. They knew what God had said."

The children's response encouraged Ken. It occurred to him that if this was good for his family, other families might like it, too. He decided to help his family and other families with a thought-for-thought translation of the Epistles—the New Testament letters from Romans to Jude.

The Taylors live in Wheaton, Illinois, a suburb twenty-five miles west of Chicago. At that time, Ken commuted to the Windy City, riding on the train an hour and a half a day. He found he could do a lot of work in that time. He also worked on the paraphrase in the evenings, using commentaries to tighten up the meanings. Because his work might be used outside the family, he decided to show it to Greek experts, getting their opinions and help.

Translating the Epistles took seven long years, and then followed crushing disappointment. Five leading publishing companies turned down the manuscript. All the companies said that nobody was interested in another translation. . . .

What followed was the classic American success story.

The Taylors made Ken's manuscript a family project. Ken Taylor borrowed money, made a deal with a printer friend to pay as the book sold, and had the book printed himself. He called it *Living Letters*. His family was the editorial department, the accounting department, and the shipping department. Young Mark, child number six, then eleven years old and now president of Tyndale House, got his start in publishing by coming home from school, pulling cartons of books out from under his bed, and sending out the day's orders.

At first Mark didn't have too much to do. The Taylors sold eight hundred copies at a booksellers' convention, where Ken shared a ten-foot booth with a man selling offering plates. Then the family waited for reorders—the crucial reorders which would let them know whether anybody out there was buying the book from the bookstore shelves. They waited one month. Two months. Three. When no reorders had come in the first four months, all looked lost. Then, finally, Mark got back to work as a trickle of orders began.

The big break came when someone gave Billy Graham a copy. He read the book with great interest and decided to give copies away on crusade telecasts. The first crusade printing was fifty thousand copies, and eventually Graham gave away half a million copies.

"At first I hadn't planned to go beyond the Epistles," Dr. Taylor recounts. "Then someone asked me, 'When are you going to do the Gospels?' I told her that the Gospels were fairly clear. 'Then maybe you can tell me what this means,' she said. 'The wind bloweth whither it listeth.' "

Ken experimented with the Gospels, and the same principles worked. When it appeared that *Living Letters* could be a commercial success, he wanted to spend full time doing the rest of the Bible. It took nine years.

"The hardest part was deciding when to risk leaving my full-time job," Ken says. "We seemed to be selling almost enough books to equal my salary. And we had no overhead. So the real question was, would the book continue to sell, or would it stop?

"I remember finally telling the family that I wasn't sure where I was going, but I knew I was on a guided tour. So I had no great trauma or fears."

Thus, in a small farmhouse on the flatlands of Illinois, home to ten children, The Living Bible took form. Ken worked at his desk in the bedroom. The Taylors moved the shipping area from under Mark's bed to a garage they bought from the Chicago, Aurora and Elgin Railroad. And when there was a mailing to do, everyone pitched in.

Certainly the Taylor family was large enough to staff a sizable business! Ken says with a grin, "All our children were planned—they just weren't all planned by Margaret and me." Raising ten children, who arrived over a fourteen-year span, required creative use of resources. The Muirs next door had five children, and the Rogers down the block had eight. So the fall and spring ritual was to visit garage sales and rummage sales and purchase shoes that were in good shape. The boxes would be passed among the three families, and each child would take shoes that fit.

Bringing up a large family is costly in time as well. "In theory and practice," says Ken, "a father should spend *personal* time with each child. Finding that kind of time to give each child is sometimes difficult, and it's even harder in a large family.

"You know, we just don't have very long. The children grow up so fast, and then it's too late."

"We went on family picnics and camp-outs and had a lot of fun with the group as a whole. But in addition, I think it's really important to spend individual time. One of my sons takes a child to breakfast every Saturday morning. Another sets aside an entire evening each week. I wish I had thought of some creative ideas like that."

Ken wishes he had realized the importance of that individual attention earlier. "You know, we just don't have very long. The children grow up so fast, and then it's too late.

"We all tend to do what our parents did. They are our models. I wish I had had more of a model." Because Ken's father didn't marry until he was forty, he was older than most fathers. Ken was the second of three brothers, one a year-and-a-half older and the other twelve years younger. While they had a good family relationship, Ken says, "I wish my father had given me more individual time.

"In fact, it's important for both fathers and mothers. Susannah Wesley had nineteen children (nine died in infancy), and it is written that she gave each child at least an hour a week of individual time."

Ken now tries to invest time in his grandchildren. "Maybe it's different with a grandchild. There are always things a kid seems to think his grandfather needs to know. It's probably the wrong idea that you need to have deep discussions. Being together is what's important."

Kenneth Taylor speaks now as both the father of a large family and the grandfather of nineteen children. One of the clan's great events is the occasional gathering at the Taylors' summer home near Lake Michigan. When as many as eight of the ten children gather with spouses and children, the rooms are filled, as are the porches and the yard. Most of the clan is usually home for Christmas, too.

It has been written that a person cannot know how well he has done with his children until he sees how his grandchildren turn out. "I see things my children are doing as parents, and it pleases me very much," says Ken. "Some of them seek my advice; others tolerate it." He grins, "They all get it."

He concedes that parents of adult children need to wait until asked to give advice. He's learned there is more than one right way to bring up a family, so he tries to be aware of what really produces a good product. He reflects, "We always had rigid bedtimes. But some of our grandchildren wander around the house half the night, and they're still turning out great."

As the parents of ten, Ken and Margaret had several age spans to deal with at the same time. Today, with the tendency toward smaller but more "spread out" families, parents have some of the same difficulties. "Flexibility is the significant word. The perspectives change as the child gets older. Several of our kids sailed through childhood and teen years with great attitudes. Others went through rough times as teens. One was a good-natured rebel. It was the personality and temperament of the child not to be happy to obey. At times a child would appear to be drifting away from the family, or becoming disillusioned with the faith, not showing the spiritual interest I would desire.

"Not every child turns out the way we hope and dream. The Lord calls each person individually; he evaluates the interests and abilities. It is dangerous for parents to say, 'I want my child to do this or be that.'"

Every time another baby came along, Margaret would say, "How can I feed this child?" Ken would say, "How can I get this child through college?" Now he says, "I was in serious error to think every kid should go to college. I used to think it was the most important thing parents could do for a child."

He doesn't feel as strongly about that now. "College is valuable for social growth and essential for some occupations, but I wouldn't make it a primary goal anymore. We used our money unwisely. I saved it for college educations instead of using it to help develop the children right then. I embarrassed some of them unnecessarily by driving around in junk cars because I was saving for college. We scrimped on vacations because we needed to save for college."

But he does remember some fine camping trips, recalling that they visited almost every campground in Michigan and Wisconsin. "Peter still talks about the time when we were camping at the Michigan dunes. We came on this house which was built on the dune, on the sand. The dunes were eroding away; the house was abandoned and starting to fall apart. What a spiritual lesson. It was just the right time, the right place, to make the point of building on a strong foundation."

Another fond memory is of a glorious trip to Colorado in an old Cadillac which had a window separating the driver and the back. "I paid $250 for it. It was quite a car! Four kids sat on the rear seat, three were in the jump seat, and the other five of us rode in the front. But that was my fallacy again. I spent almost every evening trying to find a garage to fix the car, so I didn't spend as much time as I could have with the family."

But when the Taylor children reminisce, they recall fun times they had as a family. Sometimes their parents hear stories they'd never known about before! The children's memories display the satisfaction of kids who always had someone else around to do something with.

"We believed that television intruded too much on the family."

One unusual decision of the Taylor household has been carried on by their offspring. All but one of their children are among the 1.9 percent of U.S. families who don't have television sets. TV came into widespread usage when the older children were in grade school, but the Taylors resisted for several reasons. First, they noticed that it was increasingly difficult to visit in the homes of friends because TV shows would interfere with conversation. Ken and Margaret decided that they didn't want to be addicted to the tube. "We also realized that we could be watching some subtly dangerous programs, even in those days," observes Ken. "And now it is even more true, as families have gotten used to lower standards.

"We believed that television intruded too much on the family. We realized that we were missing good programming, but on balance

155

we feared we couldn't control it without a hassle. At certain times we would rent a television, like at Christmas when there would be some good programs. And other times our kids would troop over to the neighbors."

The Taylors agree that families who don't watch TV will read more. They will play board games and will talk more.

Today Ken has a number of thoughts about family devotions, the catalyst for The Living Bible and Ken's consequent fame. "I'm concerned that so few families have this time of devotions. But if I were doing it over, I would make it more of a family time. I'd broaden it past just Bible reading and family prayer. I'd read children's classics and other stories. I'd let children in on the problems at work. I'd be sure they knew how we were coming along as a family."

Ken thinks most families can find some common time for devotions. For the Taylors, right after supper was a good time. They decided to have devotions even if just he and and his wife were present. It was a matter of deciding how important it was.

Over the years the Taylor family has changed. Gone are the days when "any day without spilled milk is a good day." Also gone is the egg route: Margaret would purchase farm-fresh eggs, and seven kids in succession delivered them to customers at a profit of ten cents per dozen. Gone are the days when Ken would wake up at night, sensing something was wrong—and then realize it was simply that one more child had left for college, leaving the household short another person. Gone also are the days when each child needed to establish his or her own identity, as when one admitted to a friend at college, "Yes, I know those Taylors from Wheaton, the ones who did The Living Bible."

Instead, Ken has grandchildren who don't really understand that Grandpa is well known—except for one little girl who saw Ken's picture on a commemorative mug and observed, "Grandpa must be famous." Instead, he has grandchildren who like to come by and talk and laugh or just sit in his waiting lap. He has adult children who are happy about what their father has accomplished, but now have found their own places in life. They are not dependent upon what someone else has done, but are making their own ways and raising their own families.

I wonder," muses Kenneth Taylor, "if my great-grandchildren will know as little about me as I know about my great-grandfather. I am now aware of how quickly we pass off the scene." To his family, Kenneth Taylor is a famous man—not because he brought the world The Living Bible, but because, for the most part, he has achieved happiness and satisfaction with his family.

FATHERLOVE

I will always remember
The baby small and warm
A universe in human form
Laying in my arms
A sweet unspoken promise;
A new life just begun
In fatherlove.

Chorus:
Daddy and daughter,
Father and son
I helped you to walk
Now, look at you run!
A tear in my eye
And thanks in my heart
For fatherlove.

Fatherlove; the legacy.
I held your mother close to me
And we shared the hope of
what's to be
Fatherlove; the child beget.
The father who is famous yet
To a child who never shall forget
His father's love.

Stookey, Toht, Lewis, and Palmer
© 1984 Neworld Media Music Publishing (ASCAP)

FAMOUS FATHERS

How to become famous with your kids.

NOW ON FILM AND VIDEOTAPE

Well-known dads Josh McDowell, Bill Gaither, Ken Cooper, Rosey Grier, Stan Smith, and Noel Paul Stookey are now appearing in a film/video series, **FAMOUS FATHERS: How to Become Famous with Your Kids.**

Four 30-minute segments feature candid home interviews with each of the men on the topics:

1) The Fatherhood Adventure—celebrating the joys of being a father.

2) The Gift of Discipline—deciding to take the job seriously.

3) The Gift of Spiritual Direction—how to nurture spiritual growth in your children.

4) The Gift of Understanding—establishing good communication with your kids.

FAMOUS FATHERS can be rented on 16mm film for large, general audiences, or purchased on videotape along with printed materials for small study groups. Either way, the series is a practical, nonthreatening way to provide Christian fathers with encouragement and challenge.

For information on the film, call 312/695-9010 and ask for Bill Tatum, or simply write to the address at the front of the book. For information on the videotape, do the same or contact your local Christian bookstore.

DADS ONLY editor Paul Lewis invites you to join the thousands of fathers across America who read DADS ONLY Newsletter. Every month, 12 pages of quick tips and ideas help you to stay famous with your kids.

For more information, write:
DADS ONLY
P.O. Box 340
Julian, CA 92036